Grimoire of Magical Inks

"The next time you do spell work, draw talismans or sigils, inscribe ritual tools, sign oaths or certificates, or record entries in your magical journal, personal grimoire, or book of shadows, consult Noémie Myara's *Grimoire of Magical Inks* first for inspiration on how to elevate one of the most easily overlooked items in your toolkit."

RICHARD KACZYNSKI, AUTHOR OF
MIND OVER MAGICK

"Noémie Myara has a rare gift for making a specialized craft feel inviting, and *Grimoire of Magical Inks* is proof—the definitive guide that meets you exactly where you are in your practice. Never overwhelming, never oversimplifying, it's a book any practitioner can learn from."

MADISON LILLIAN, CO-OWNER OF SPELLCRAFTER,
A METAPHYSICAL AND WITCHCRAFT STORE

"If, like me, you have never thought of making magical inks before, this expert author will inspire you to grab a few simple ingredients and make some immediately. Powerful spells, powerful recipes, powerful magic! Highly recommended."

CAIT JOHNSON, AUTHOR OF
WITCH WISDOM FOR MAGICAL AGING AND
WITCH IN THE KITCHEN

Grimoire of Magical Inks

Recipes for Hexes, Hoodoo, and High Magic

Noémie Myara

Translated by Jon E. Graham

DESTINY BOOKS
ROCHESTER, VERMONT

Destiny Books
One Park Street
Rochester, Vermont 05767
www.DestinyBooks.com

Destiny Books is a division of Inner Traditions International

Originally published in French in 2024 under the title *Grimoire des encres magique* by Éditions Bussière
First U.S. edition published in 2026 by Destiny Books

Cataloging-in-Publication Data for this title is available from the Library of Congress

ISBN 979-8-88850-523-6 (print)
ISBN 979-8-88850-524-3 (ebook)

Printed and bound in China by Reliance Printing Co., Ltd.

10 9 8 7 6 5 4 3 2 1

Text design and layout by Kenleigh Manseau
This book was typeset in Garamond Premier Pro with Gotham, Sepian, and P22 Morris used as display typefaces

Freepik illustration credits: © Incroforman; © rawpixel.com; © pikisuperstar; © ArtsparLeila; © Brelena; © macrovecteur; © azerbaijan_stockers; © asrulaqroni; © Tohamina; © vlada1294; © Racool_studio; © brgfx; © memajflorin; © mutia_paint; © Rojkova_jil; © liska5; © SkorStock; © brelena; © memajflorin; © solutionlawson; © aleksaal; © 3DdarkZone. CC BY-SA 4.0: pages 15, 43, and 130.

To send correspondence to the author of this book, mail a first-class letter to the author c/o Inner Traditions, One Park Street, Rochester, VT 05767, and we will forward the communication.

Contents

Introduction
Entering the World of Magical Inks

Ink is something with which we are all familiar. Most of us know ink from using it in its standard form since childhood, but few people are aware of its magical dimension. Inks have been tools and allies of witches and wizards since time immemorial. From drawing symbols to various divination practices, in addition to its use as a tool in everyday life, ink has been a valuable partner for numerous practitioners from an array of art, magic, and esoteric traditions.

In this book, I will offer detailed information about everything connected to inks and their use in the field of witchcraft and sorcery. The occult world is vast and there are many esoteric traditions (High Magic, Hoodoo, Wicca, Druidry, Seiðr, and so on) in which magical inks are used. You should be aware that in this book I am primarily drawing from my personal eclectic practice, fed by various esoteric schools of thought and occult practices. I will happily share my knowledge with you about magical inks and how I use them in my practices.

We will look at what are known as magical inks and what they are used for, and how to make them and ritually consecrate them for use in witchcraft. I will also demonstrate how to use them in more traditional ways as well as through various methods for divination, spellcasting, and magical creations. First and foremost, this book is my own personal sharing, one that I hope will allow you to discover new things and enrich your own magic practice. I wish you an enjoyable read.

NOÉMIE

One
Magical Inks

HISTORY AND GENERAL INFORMATION

Ink's history goes very far back in time. The earliest traces of works made with ink or a substance quite similar to it have been found in caves. Some of these vestiges of the remote past go back to the Neanderthal era, in other words 50,000 years ago. Even if they cannot be considered "inks" as we understand them today, the black and ochre colors of cave art can be considered to be their foundations and origins.

Several different uses of ink have been discovered throughout the course of history in many ancient cultures that developed it from plants, minerals, and animal products. We can see how ink was used in ancient Egypt thanks to the papyri written by the scribes. The Egyptians mastered several pigmentation techniques: Their inks contained charcoal and pigments of plant and mineral origin. The same was true in India and China. In the Tian Mountains of the latter during the reign of Huangdi (2697 BC), ink was a kind of lacquer that was applied to silk with a piece of bamboo before being replaced by a black stone (an ink stick) that had to be dipped into water beforehand and rubbed. The well-known Chinese or Indian ink, whose original base was a black carbon pigment, was made from a fluid binding agent (such as protein, skin, or fish glue). This was followed by the use of plant-based glues, which were useful because of their tanning effect and for creating ink that was indelible.

While it is most often liquid, ink can also come in the form of a paste. As a general rule, its current composition includes a base of water, resin, pigments or dyes, and solvents. But it is also possible to manufacture your own natural inks thanks to recipes that you can find further on in this book. Ink has the distinctive feature of being colored for the purpose of leaving a mark on the surface to which it is applied. Depending on their intended use (drawing, printing, and so forth), and the surface on which they are to be used (paper, ceramics, skin, and so forth), there are different kinds of ink. There are also different methods and tools for using ink: pens, brushes, needles, fingers, and so on.

FLUIDIC CAPACITORS IN WITCHCRAFT

Magical inks are considered to be fluidic capacitors or condensers, similar to other allies in witchcraft rituals. First you may ask, just what is a *fluidic capacitor* in witchcraft? This is a term found in occult practices for describing an energy conductor that has a strong ability to capture, store, charge, amplify, and transmit magical energies. Several ancient, magical works mention them, but many contemporary authors and occultists also lay claim to their use. The term *fluidic* does not necessarily mean that the capacitor is liquid; it refers to vital energy, a charge of energy, or the flow of magical energy.

Simply by virtue of its function a fluidic capacitor is already a powerful ally. For this reason, a sorcerer or a witch will create a fluid condenser like this to store the properties, qualities, and magic of the natural elements that go into its composition as well as their own intentions and outside influences (such as those of stars, spirits, deities, and so on). He or she will then charge it with a ritual and use it during specific circumstances for casting spells. As you can see, a fluidic capacitor is a decisive ally that gives you the power to master different kinds of energy. It is a proven and major tool for working magic.

The substances used to create these energy condensers can be solid, liquid, or gaseous. We find among the standard traditional elements that can be crafted and charged ritually to become fluidic capacitors. These include incense made from natural resins and plants, plant or beeswax, metals, oils, essential oils, perfumes, sprays, and of course inks.

Magical inks are attributed a distinctive (and not at all negligible) character in several esoteric practices in comparison to other fluidic capacitors. They in fact symbolize blood and vital fluids in magic analogies. One of the most powerful condensers of the flow of vital energy is blood, so it may often be added to magical inks to make them much more effective. Don't let this creep you out. We will revisit it in greater detail on page 49 when we touch on an equally important subject: witnesses.

WHAT ARE MAGICAL INKS?

A magical ink is an ink that has been consecrated for use in the practice of magic, a purpose for which it has been ritualized. This ink can be made by hand or bought in a store that sells occult items. It is also possible to use traditional ink, such as India ink, by customizing it before ritually consecrating it. But we will also look at how to make your own inks from scratch.

Inks that have been consecrated for magic use are generally used to draw symbols, sigils, seals, and runes; to write magic words; or to spell out the intentions that shape the incantation or charm to be cast. They can also play a role in the crafting of various creations such as magic salts, spell jars, amulets, and talismans.

These magical inks can be used in a wide variety of spells, rituals, and practices, and there are numerous ways to use them. They are helpful for completing your grimoire (or book of shadows), to spread over sacred symbols that have been carved on candles, to mark fabric, to draw on the body, to practice automatic or intuitive writing, to block a mirror or a spell, to write and sign occult pacts, among other things. To sum it up, inks have a choice place in all magical acts.

They do stand out from the standard tools intended for witchcraft rituals. However, they are essential elements in certain divination practices such as those that involve interpreting the shapes made by ink on different mediums like on papers (inkromancy) or in water. This latter method is not so well known, and we will revisit it in greater detail later in the book. Personally, what I love about inks is their versatility in many different uses and functions.

I like to save inks for specific magical operations. As I view them as a magical tool, this is a way for amplifying their power. By saving an ink for a very specific task, I accentuate its unique qualities in my practice and the power it brings to the role it has to play. I like to ritualize them and create them with a definite purpose in mind as this enhances their efficacy in the magic they bring to the purpose for which they have been crafted. This is one of the reasons why I am offering you so many recipes, not only does this give you a larger array to choose from but you will be more likely to find the one that speaks to you most deeply and will best serve your needs. And if, like me, you want several inks for specific purposes in your rituals or divination practices, you will be able to do so with no problem.

Two

Crafting Your Own Ink

In this part of the book we are going to look at how to create inks using different plant recipes.

THE BASICS

Here we are going to discover several recipes for manufacturing various colored inks. I should clearly state here that the gum arabic (also known as acacia resin) used to make the inks in the following recipes is not in its traditional form of grains. Here we use gum arabic in concentrated liquid form, which can be readily found in art supply and other specialty stores. It is a natural binding agent with a multitude of uses. In the event you are only able to find raw gum arabic, it is possible to grind it into a very fine powder that can be mixed into your preparations.

I recommend that you store your ink in an opaque glass container—either a bottle or a jar—that has an airtight lid. Ink will also last much longer in a container that has been sterilized beforehand with boiling water. This is because, yes, homemade ink is a natural product that can begin to mold over time.

To stabilize your ink and give it a longer shelf life, I have another tip to share with you: You can add a couple drops of alcohol (such as 80 proof vodka) or white vinegar. You can also use certain essential oils, which will also have the bonus of adding fragrance to your ink.

COLORED INK RECIPES

A large variety of plants can be used to craft magical inks, and their roots, nuts, berries, and other parts are all good for this purpose. They all can be used as the raw materials for both creating inks, as we are about to see, and for customizing inks, as we will see later.

Black Ink

Here are two recipes for black ink—the standard color that is most often used both traditionally and in witchcraft. Black ink is suitable for all kinds of magical work.

Method 1

Ingredients

- Plants, nuts, berries, and roots. You will need to burn them in order to obtain a plant-based ash. Refer to the list on page 44 for examples of the different things you can harvest or gather based on the occult purpose your magic ally will fulfill.
- Something to burn your plants and roots
- A pestle
- Water (preferably spring water, or sun water, or moon water), or gum arabic or vegetable oil, all of which will give your ashes a watery consistency

Preparation

Burn the dried plant matter, nuts, and/or berries until they turn to ash.

Once they have been cooled, collect the ashes and grind them into a very fine powder.

Next mix your powder with a little water, gum arabic, or vegetable oil—enough to obtain a watery consistency.

Once you have achieved the consistency you are looking for, pour your ink into a container.

Method 2

Ingredients

- ½ teaspoon of carbon black (although not quite the same, the soot known as lamp black can also be used). Carbon black is a carbonaceous residue obtained by burning organic matter with a high carbon content. It is sold as a pigment, but an acceptable substitute can be made at home using, for example, soot and charcoal ash.
- 1 egg yolk
- 1 teaspoon of gum arabic
- 5 tablespoons of honey

Preparation

Mix the egg yolk and honey together with the gum arabic.

Add the carbon black. This will produce a thick paste that you can store in an airtight container.

Mix this paste with a little water until you obtain the

desired consistency. In this method, I recommend that you keep your ink in the paste form and only dilute what you need in small amounts when you need it. However, if you want to store it in the form of a fluid ink, then make it without the egg yolk but add more gum arabic.

Red Ink

This is an ink whose base is made from pokeweed berries (Phytolacca), a plant that is widespread and relatively easy to find. However, you have to be extra careful as this plant is considered to be one of the "poisonous ladies." Although it is generally safe to be handled lightly (just to be safe, wash your hands after contact or wear gloves when handling it), the berries, roots, and seeds (the most toxic part) are not edible and should never be eaten. Red-colored ink has a symbolic meaning that can enhance all your rituals connected to the domains of emotion, love, and sexuality.

For those concerned about working with pokeweed berries, there are other nontoxic red berries that can provide the same results: chokecherries, serviceberries, and spicebush berries.

Ingredients

- Pokeweed berries (a large handful, picked one by one)
- 1 teaspoon of white vinegar or alcohol, or several drops of essential oil to help preserve your ink
- Gum arabic
- A salad bowl
- An airtight container for storing the ink

Preparation

Mash the berries in a salad bowl until pureed and begin to release their juice.

Heat this puree in a small saucepan over low heat until it comes to a boil, then take it off the heat and let stand until cool.

Filter your mixture through a fine mesh strainer or sieve while smashing the pulp. This will give you a concentrated, slightly thick liquid.

Add the spoonful of vinegar (or alcohol, essential oil, or gum arabic), and stir.

Filter the ink to obtain a thick paste and let it cool before storing it in your airtight glass bottle or jar.

Brown Ink

Brown ink is a ready alternative to black ink and can be made without charcoal or carbon black. It is also easily adapted for all kinds of magical workings.

Ingredients

- 4 teaspoons of loose tea leaves or 4 or 5 teabags
- 1 teaspoon of gum arabic
- ½ cup of boiling water

Preparation

Let the tea steep in the boiling water for around fifteen minutes.

Squeeze the tea (the tannin) as much as possible.

Incorporate the gum arabic and mix it into the tea until you have obtained a homogenous solution.

Filter the ink to obtain a thick paste and let it cool before storing it in your airtight glass bottle or jar.

Violet Ink

Ink made from blackberries produces a dark purple or blue color. It is very simple to make and consists entirely of natural material. Violet is the color of divination, making this the perfect ink to accompany your divinatory rituals, sessions, and works.

Ingredients

- 1 cup of blackberries
- ½ cup of water
- ½ teaspoon of gum arabic
- 5 drops of thyme oil

Preparation

First heat the blackberries in the water, then press on the pulp to extract the juice.

Once the mixture has become dark in color and all the juice released, filter it and then stir in the gum arabic, stirring until it has become a thick paste.

Add the thyme oil and stir. Let the ink cool before putting it in a jar or bottle.

Blue Ink

With elderberries, you can make an ink whose color will vary from blue to purple depending on the recipes. To be completely honest, it never really comes out the same color. Sometimes it can be an indigo blue or more often a dark violet. This is also a recipe that is completely natural. Elderberries produce anthocyanins. These are blue-violet pigments found in plants.

Ingredients

- 1 quart of elderberry juice or whole elderberries. You can buy quarts of black elderberry juice directly from stores or follow the recipe below to make your own if you have fresh berries.
- 2–3 bags of black tea
- 8–10 grams of powdered alum
- 8–10 grams of gum arabic

Preparation

Crush the berries in a little water, then add two teabags. Black tea is high in tannins and this substance helps set the color.

Leave it to macerate for a day so that the fruits release their juices.

Filter the macerated mixture and reduce it by bringing it to a boil over moderate heat.

Add the powdered alum and the gum arabic.

Mix everything together and let it reduce until you obtain the desired consistency.

Let it cool.

Pour it into a glass container.

OIL PAINTS

Even though oil paints are technically not inks, knowing how to make them and being familiar with a number of natural pigments that are easy to obtain will prove to be helpful if you wish to make magical drawings or paintings as is common in a number of talismanic creations. For example, we find in the hermetic tradition the use of magical symbols and seals with specific colors that are used to convey defined meanings and intentions.

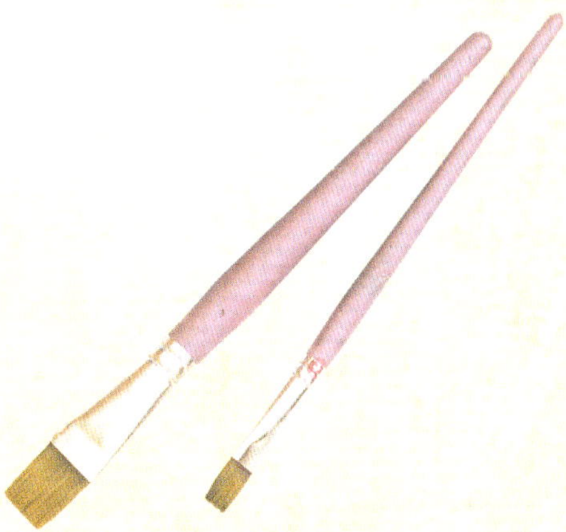

Let's take as our example the Pentacle of Earth from the Hermetic Order of the Golden Dawn created by the famous Aleister Crowley (1875–1947).

Like all magic seals, it consists of several elements: a hexagram, holy or magic words (with a space left for the adept's magical device), and a precise color code.

So, in order to have alternatives to meet your needs, here is an example of a recipe for making your own natural oil paint, which is quite simple! For this one, I am going to use curry powder, which will be the natural pigment of the recipe. But depending on the color you wish to obtain, you can choose another spice or a mineral pigment like mica or chromium oxide.

Making Oil Paint

Material

- Curry powder for the natural pigment
- Walnut oil
- A plate for mixing ingredients together
- A spatula
- A dropper

Preparation

Make a small pile of the pigment material on a plate and form a small hole in the middle, a little like a volcano.

Add a few drops of the oil at a time to the amount of pigment material until you reach approximately 30 percent oil by volume. Mix the oil in gradually until you reach the desired consistency. All pigments will not react the same way, as they will absorb the oil differently. If the mixture still seems a little too pasty, add more oil, but not too much or it will become too runny.

If you want a uniform mixture without lumps, you can use a glass muller to really crush the pigments. It is very important to make sure everything is well blended to avoid the paint cracking after application.

For better preservation of your paint, you can use a piece of aluminum foil, a small airtight jar, or even a reusable paint tube. You can also use the airtight paint palettes with trays that are airtight when closed.

Three

Turning Your Ink into a Magical Ally

First and foremost, you are the one that will make your ink magical. Whether you have personally created your ink or not, it is important to know that its "transformation" through a ritual is what will make your ink magical. Whether you begin with ink you have crafted yourself or ink that you have bought from a store, we are going to turn it into an ally in your practice of witchcraft. We will start with the personalizing or transformation of your ink, followed by the ritual of consecration that will make it sacred and imbued with magic.

THE COLORS AND THEIR MAGIC

I love to get deep into the details, and while there are no hard, fast rules on this subject, I personally work a lot with symbolism. Symbolism holds a primordial role in the esoteric sciences. It is important to take this into account when preparing to work magic.

Colors have always held great meaning in witchcraft and the occult world, and each is loaded with symbolism, function, and power. In many ways, like when directing your energy and intention during a ritual, possessing certain information will be valuable to you.

A color is a symbol in itself, since, like all symbols, it evokes or refers to something. This often falls into the domain of the abstract, in which we most often set an emotion, a belief, a form of energy, a value, a power, or an intention.

Let's take the example of pink. This color represents gentleness, love, tenderness, femininity, and flowers. Or red, which stands for passion, love, sexuality, or, like pink, it can also represent the flower, the rose.

This shows that two different colors can share some of the same symbolism or, in some way, intersect.

It is important to realize that our perceptions of a symbol and what it inspires will be influenced by our personal values, our personal beliefs, and our own culture.

When using inks for practicing magic, I personally tend to use the colors black, red, and purple. So, I will start by sharing with you the symbolism of these colors before discussing others.*

*Beyond the category of inks, any knowledge about color magic will be useful for all your magical workings.

The Symbolism of Black

Commonly, the color black refers to death, mourning, evil, nothingness, and emptiness. These beliefs may be based on a fear of the dark (shared by all children), or just on fear in general. I won't delve into an in-depth analysis but we have to admit that black (mourning, sorrow, dirtiness, evil) is traditionally opposed to white (purity, innocence, good). In reality, like all colors, black is neither good nor bad. It assumes many symbolic meanings depending on the context, domain, culture, and belief system.

I would like to offer you here a few correspondences of the color black in esoteric practice. This will allow you to determine what best suits your own beliefs, associations, and intentions, and thus to take ownership of your own symbolic and magical correspondences.

For example, I find black ink to be perfect for rituals, spells, and divination practices in the areas of protection, grounding, banishment, and mediumship (contact with the afterlife, ancestors, certain deities, and so forth).

Correspondences of Black

- Moon phase: New moon
- Planets: Pluto, Saturn
- Sabbat: Samhain
- Chakra: Root
- Element: Earth
- Season: Winter

- Direction: North
- Energy: Yin
- Deities: Hecate, Hades, Bastet, Anubis, Thoth, Lilith, Kali, Krishna, the Morrigan, Odin, Hel, Loki

Magical and Spiritual Uses

Everything that is connected to the following areas:

- Protection, banishment
- Counter-spells
- Defensive magic
- Enchantment
- Psychic abilities
- Divination
- Mediumship
- Contact with subtle worlds, the afterlife, the deceased
- Magic related to the dead, mourning, ancestors
- Magic of the night and the nocturnal world, dreams, the astral plane
- Liberation rituals
- Work on anger, grief, renewal, transformation, negativity, fears, letting go

The Symbolism of Purple

When it comes to shades of purple there is a fairly wide range. From light mauve to indigo, purple leaves no one indifferent. It is a color rich in spirituality and esotericism, endowed with symbolism that can range from soft and luminous to darker and more severe. Personally, I find purple to be the most appropriate color for everything related to dreams, consciousness, spirituality, or wisdom. As well as to spells, rituals, and symbols related to the divinatory arts, contact with our guides, mediumship, clairvoyance, and intuition.

Correspondences of Purple

- Moon phases: all
- Planets: Neptune, Uranus, Saturn
- Sabbats: Ostara, Beltane, Samhain
- Season: Spring
- Elements: Water and Air
- Chakras: Third Eye and Crown
- Deities: Tyr, Iris, Circe, Shiva, Apollo, Persephone, Hera, Nephthys
- Magical and spiritual uses: Everything associated with the realms of wisdom, spirituality, consciousness, awakening, connection to oneself and the divine, the astral and other higher planes, psychic abilities, divinatory arts, medi-

tation, concentration, transformation, healing, creativity, dreaming, the astral plane, well-being, sensitivity, introspection, and melancholy

The Symbolism of Red

Akin to some of the interpretations associated with the color black, the symbolic meanings linked to the color red are sometimes paradoxical. Red can be associated with the fires of hell, anger, war, danger, unspeakable sins, and demons. It is also the symbol of energy, life, vitality, excitement, warmth, love, passion, and sex. It was one of the first pigments to be mastered. As early as the Paleolithic era, first with ochre earth, then with madder, and finally with metals.* Red has been one of the "basic" colors since ancient times.

For my part, red ink is what I use for workings related to love and sexuality.

Correspondences of Red

- Chakras: Root and Sacral
- Deities: Aphrodite, Ares, Persephone, Freyja, Venus, Mars, Brahma, Ganesh, Thor, Seth, Isis, Lilith, Vulcan/Hephaestus
- Direction: South
- Element: Fire

*Madder is a plant with dye-producing roots and metals used included iron oxide and mercury sulfide.

- Magical and spiritual uses: Everything that is related to the realms of aggressivity, strength, action, willpower, courage, love, sexuality, desire, masculinity and femininity, enchantment, vitality, fire, roots, protection, healing, power, revenge, and anger
- Moon phases: Full moon, waxing moon
- Planets: Sun, Mars, Venus
- Sabbats: Beltane, Litha, Lughnasadh, Mabon, Samhain, Yule

The Symbolism of Orange

Blending red and yellow together, orange is a dynamic and invigorating color that often symbolizes joy and optimism. A gentler hue than red, the features symbolized by orange are often "reassuring."

Correspondences of Orange

- Celestial bodies: Sun, Mars, Mercury
- Deities: Hestia, Mithra, Lug, Freya, Vulcan/Hephaestus, Zeus, Odin, Thor
- Seasons: Summer, Fall
- Sabbats: Beltane, Litha, Lughnasadh, Mabon, Samhain
- Element: Fire
- Chakra: Sacral and Solar Plexus

- Magical and spiritual uses: Everything related to joy, vitality, fire, optimism, creativity, abundance, attraction, ambition, expansion, self-confidence, change, warmth, kindness, healing, achievement, success, and travel

The Symbolism of Yellow or Gold

Yellow was esteemed throughout antiquity by many cultures because of its frequent association with gold. It embodied power, success, and wealth. But gold may also mean conflict when it comes to wealth and treasure. Gold and yellow are therefore also linked to betrayal, deception, lies, and treachery.

Correspondences of Yellow

- Planets: Sun, Mercury
- Sabbats: Ostara, Beltane, Litha, Lughnasadh, Mabon
- Elements: Air, Fire
- Direction: East
- Chakra: Solar Plexus
- Deities: Helios, Mithra, Ra, Maat, Sarasvati, Lug, Ganesh, Zeus, Odin, Frejya, Vulcan, Hephaestus, Cernunnos
- Magical and spiritual uses: Everything connected with healing, joy, success, prosperity, energy, the sun, willpower, strength, positivity, home, and security

The Symbolism of Green

Green is evocative of nature and therefore life. Although it is the color of hope and luck in many traditions, it is also one of those colors with opposing meanings. It is generally forbidden in theaters because it allegedly invites bad luck. This superstition may simply have arisen from the rumor that the famous French playwright Molière died in the middle of a performance of one of his plays while wearing a green coat.

Correspondences of Green

- Planet: Earth
- Sabbats: Imbolc, Ostara, Beltane, Yule
- Element: Earth
- Chakra: Heart
- Deities: Ostara, Osiris, Iris, Hathor, Horus, Gaia, Cernunnos, Brigit, Pan, Faunus, Ganesh

- Magical and spiritual uses: Everything related to abundance, luck, compassion, money, nature and nature spirits, acceptance, hope, travel, kindness, healing, fertility, and home

The Symbolism of Blue

Although it is an extremely common color, blue is not easy to produce naturally. The first shades of blue were created from minerals—lapis lazuli in this instance—as recorded in hieroglyphic texts in ancient Egypt. A plant known as woad also makes it possible to create this hue.

Correspondences of Blue

- Planets: Moon, Neptune, Earth
- Sabbats: Ostara, Beltane, Litha, Yule
- Elements: Water, Air
- Directions: East & West
- Chakra: Throat
- Deities: Ganesh, Krishna, Amun, Nut, Athena
- Magical and spiritual uses: Everything that has a connection with communication, intellect, exchange, happiness, emotions, harmony, sleep, peace, health, spirituality, and balance

The Symbolism of Brown

Although present everywhere in nature, the color brown is not as well liked as green. In popular belief it is often associated with filth, poverty, and ugliness. However, it is the color of earth and has a place in many beautiful things, especially in the esoteric domain.

Correspondences of Brown

- Sabbats: Lughnasadh (reddish brown), Mabon
- Planets: Saturn, Earth
- Deities: Cernunnos, Faunus, Pan, Gaia, Brigit, Geb
- Element: Earth
- Chakra: Root
- Magical and spiritual uses: Everything related to the realms of grounding, earth, nature, animals (especially their protection), home, protection, rebirth, healing, stability, and travel

The Symbolism of Gray or Silver

This color is a skillful blend of white and black. In our time gray is often associated with sorrow, melancholy, boredom, or even growing old. But in magic, this color symbolizes wisdom, knowledge, the mysteries, and the intellect (the famous gray matter).

Correspondences of Gray

- Planets: Mercury, Moon
- Element: Air
- Direction: West
- Deities: Hecate, Thoth, Selene, Artemis, Skadi, Áine
- Sabbats: Samhain, Yule
- Magical and spiritual uses: Everything that has a connection with the realms of wisdom, midheaven, the subtle planes. Protection, defense, humility, piety, secrets, the dream worlds and dreams, sorrow, melancholy, loneliness, the mind, visions, the ancestors, the old ones, the past, intuition, and moon rituals.

The Symbolism of Pink or Rose

I've held one of the sweetest colors for last. Often synonymous with love, gentleness, romanticism, and femininity, it could be described, if I may put it this way, as a "sugarcoated" version of red or at least it represents all the good aspects of that color.

Correspondences of Pink

- Planet: Venus
- Sabbats: Ostara, Beltane
- Chakra: Heart
- Deities: Aphrodite, Venus, Hathor, Freyja, Isis, Ishtar, Idunn, Frigg
- Magical and spiritual uses: Everything associated with the domains of love, charm, romanticism, attraction, gentleness, affection, friendship, happiness, beauty, compassion, emotions, and harmony

THE TRANSFORMATION OF INK INTO A MAGIC ALLY

In its standard form, "simple" ink is the basis for magical ink. Up to here, we have looked at everything concerning ink from the perspective of its history and creation. Now we will examine the magic of ink.

As we have seen, colors accentuate specific intentions in accordance with their symbolism. The same holds true for the ingredients that are added to the standard ink base.

You can always purchase ready-to-use magic ink for your magical practices in occult or new age shops. You can still add your own personal touch and, if necessary, an additional witness (see p. 49).

But what can a witch add to ink to make it magical?

Well, all sorts of things, which I invite you to discover before we move on to ritualization. Let's dive into the most magical pages of this book!

Ashes

Among the ingredients you can add to ink to enhance its magical power, there are traditionally ashes, especially ashes that come from the mixtures of plants and natural resins.

You should choose them according to your intentions for the ritual, as well as your beliefs, desires, and esoteric practices.

Simply burn the chosen plants or resins using hot coals (the same ones you use to light incense) and collect the ashes, which you will then mix with your ink. If the plants and resins do not burn completely, feel free to reduce the residue to a powder using a mortar. In theory, it is not absolutely necessary to reduce the plants to ashes, but doing so will make your ink more effective.

Well-prepared ashes dissolve better in ink (and also ensure better ink preservation), making it easier to use as there are no lumps or plant particles that could interfere with writing or divination.

To create effective ink, use approximately one teaspoon of ashes for every 20 to 30 ml of ink.

Ashes symbolize both existing matter and what is no longer matter. Ash brings together and connects the visible and the invisible, the material and the abstract, the finite and the infinite. It therefore most likely helps to strengthen your fluidic capacitor.

It is important to always shake your bottle of magic ink well before use to ensure it is homogeneous and to reenergize its magic.

Here is a short list of commonly used plants and resins.

The Resins

Acacia resin: This resin is the one recommended most often. I mentioned it when discussing the ingredients for making natural inks. It is also known as acacia gum or gum arabic. As a symbol of rebirth, immortality, and spiritual victory, acacia accentuates mediumistic powers and brings inspiration into the spiritual domain. This plant also has great healing properties. Its resin (or gum) is used to make ink, particularly for high magic rituals, for its ability to increase beneficial and subtle vibrations. It stimulates the magician's faculties and reinforces the power of prayer. It amplifies intuition and mental strength. This plant can be burned during meditation sessions to more easily capture messages from the invisible world.

Red Myrrh resin: Nicknamed "the perfume of mystics," myrrh has a very singular aura. Linked to many civilizations since the dawn of time, myrrh has always been considered sacred in the arid regions of Africa and the Middle East. It is a purifying agent and increases the power of resins and other plants with which it is associated. Widely used in magic, it establishes balance among different energies. The Egyptians believed it came from the tears of Horus and burned it as an offering to the god Ra. Its fragrance stimulates sensuality. It is found in various forms of magic, some of which are related to love. It is also a resin used as an offering. Black myrrh resin can also be used in the same way as the red.

Dragon's Blood resin: This resin extracted from the dragon tree (*Dracaena draco*) is used for purifying and banishing spells. Depending on the spell, it can either attract or repel. It increases the effects of the magic, spells, and elements with which it is mixed.

Cape aloe resin: This resin is used to drive away all kinds of negative entities. It purifies and cleanses energetically. Very powerful, it can be used on people, as well as on objects or places. It is used in rituals to break enchantments, to craft protection spells, and to ward off the evil eye. In divination, it promotes connection to the subtle planes. It can be used as an offering.

Frankincense (or olibanum): This very powerful purifier makes it possible to dispel negative energies and cleanse objects, places, and even the aura. It is a valuable tool in all kinds of rituals and consecrations. It promotes the development of spiritual awareness. It is the preeminent incense for any and all magical work as it amplifies the other elements in an incense blend and is also used as an offering.

Sandalwood: Both the bark and resin of this sacred tree can be used. Sandalwood is very useful for cleansing and energy purification, for protection, meditation, healing, developing mental power, stabilizing emotions, spiritual quests, and elevation.

Storax resin: This dark resin provides protection, constancy, and balance. It purifies memories and is used in exorcisms to drive demons out.

Pine resin: Pine is one of the nine sacred trees in Celtic tradition and its resin is used for protection, grounding, and spells of virility, fertility, and protection. Its resin can also be used to repel evil spells back to their sender and to purify people and places. It also offers valuable assistance in healing rituals.

Copal resin: This resin helps to awaken awareness or achieve higher states of consciousness that are conducive to meditation. Thanks to its purifying and protective properties, copal can also be used for energy cleansing. It protects those present and helps them to get rid of any potential negative vibes surrounding them.

Dammar resin (or gum): Also known as cat-eye resin, this resin lifts the spirit and brings light to the darkness of the soul. Used for introspection, it also brings inspiration, clarifies the mind, and promotes clear-sightedness.

Benzoin resin: Benzoin has purifying properties. It also promotes intellectual activity in addition to calming and soothing the mind. It is an important protector and purifier. Different types of benzoin exist, which are often used for rituals of purification, protection, luck, prosperity, and personal growth.

Plants

Here are a few recommended plants that are good for personalizing your inks and making them magical:

Rose: This flower is ideal for rituals involving love, friendship, passion, gentleness, beauty, sensuality, charm, and healing. It is also associated with several goddesses of love. It can be used as a substitute for other flowers in magical preparations.

Lavender: This flower soothes the mind, channels thoughts, and encourages mental activity. It also purifies and drives negative energy away.

Mugwort: This plant develops clairvoyance, dream work, and establishes a connection to the astral plane. It helps fight black magic. It is an ally that helps the witch cast counter-spells, as well as spells of defensive magic, and protection.

Cedar: This tree helps the spell caster fight evil spells and chase away demons. It is used in banishing rituals, protects, purifies, and brings healing, strength, and abundance.

Jasmine: This plant embodies calm, inner peace, and love's tenderness. Its sweet and captivating fragrance generates sensual even carnal warmth. It is used in incense and creations related to love, desire, sensuality, gentleness, well-being, gentleness, and light. This plant is also used in divination.

Mallow: This plant is associated with the moon and things feminine; this plant is often used in divination because it stimulates the third eye and the crown chakra. It therefore promotes clairvoyance and clear, premonitory dreams.

Sage: This herb is used for protection and energy cleansing. Sage brings healing and drives negative energies or entities away. It should not be used alone, as it opens invisible doors, which allows entities to enter and leave as they will!

Burdock: Which is also known as the "herb for scabies," is a plant whose root has powerful protective and healing properties and is used in magic as a purifying plant. It wards off negative influences and is very useful in spells designed to chase away nightmares and promote restful sleep.

Honeysuckle: This plant is ideal for love bonds. It stimulates psychic powers and connection to the earth and emotions.

Mint: This herb is used for healing, love, luck, and protection. Mint drives away negative energies, making room for new, positive energies.

Rosemary: This herb is one of the oldest plants used in smudging and suffumigation, particularly for the purpose of purification and protection. It can be used as a substitute for many other plants when necessary.

Lemon balm: This herb's leaves are frequently used in rituals for healing, love, or success. Lemon balm wards off evil spirits. It is prized in magic for its strong positive vibrations.

Valerian: The soporific properties of this plant's roots link it to the magic of the dream world, dreams, and sleep. Associated with the feminine, this protective plant is useful for magic concerning love or libido. It is also an essential ally in the divinatory arts as it encourages psychic gifts.

Licorice: The magical properties of this root encourage contact with ancestors. It lifts the veil, allowing you to feel or see ghostly presences. It can also be used in magic related to love and sexual desire, as it fuels passion.

Clove: This spice wards off evil spirits and stabilizes the aura. It is therefore used in rituals for protection, grounding, and divination. A symbol of purity, purification, and protection, it is also sometimes used in magical acts of luck and sexual magic.

Hawthorn: The hawthorn tree has been associated with witchcraft since time immemorial. This plant is primarily used to repel evil spells. A symbol of purity, purification, and protection, it is also sometimes used for magical works to bring luck and in sex magic.

Star anise (*badian*): This plant wards off the evil eye and provides protection. Associated with luck and Jupiter, the planet of expansion and prosperity, it is found in various spells, but also in the form of a talisman to bring good luck.

Angelica root: This is also known as angel herb or archangelica. These names come from its association with archangels, and it is said to ward off the devil. It is therefore a very useful plant for exorcisms. In magic, it is used against black magic and evil spirits, to promote visions, self-confidence, self-esteem, and to help us return to our roots. Native Americans traditionally use it to promote good luck by simply carrying angelica root in their pockets.

Gentian root: The root of this plant is believed to have protective powers, but it is most often used for rituals and love spells, gaining reciprocal affection, protection from strong passion, and so forth. It is almost like the plant version of rock crystal because it strengthens the powers and properties of the other plants with which it is combined. It acts as a catalyst; every ingredient that is brought into contact with it can have its active property doubled or tripled in power.

Tips

It is possible to collect the ashes from just one resin or plant for your magic ink recipes (one is the minimum required to make a standard ink). However, it is best to use at least four plants to create powerful synergies.

Take some time to think about the synergies (combinations) you want to create.

You can base your choices on different types of magical correspondences:

- Work with key numbers that have meaning for you (for example, four ingredients, one for each element: earth, air, water, fire).
- Add additional ingredients, such as a plant whose symbolism is associated with the desired synergy, or a resin linked to a deity related to your issue.

To sum up: Choose your plants and resins based on the magical correspondences, your intentions, and what you intend to use your ink for.

Witnesses

In witchcraft, a "witness" is a "secret" or "key" ingredient that allows you to act on a target from a distance or direct energy on subtle planes.

The witness must be added to your preparation of plant ashes and resins.

Some people consider its addition optional. The choice is yours, but I consider its use essential.

There are different types of witnesses that can be grouped into two families: false witnesses and true witnesses (traditionally used for the type of magic I propose in this book).

False Witnesses

Also known as "substitute witnesses," these witnesses are intended to replace witnesses that are hard to obtain. The use of false witnesses is common practice in modern witchcraft, especially when the spell does not concern the caster(s) directly. A false witness can be a photo, or a piece of paper or parchment bearing the person's first and last name and date of birth, or even the information written on the back of the photo if you are able to collect everything. This witness will be effective in its action, but it will work less quickly since the instruction will come from more ethereal planes such as the Astral or the Mental. Of course, to add it to your inks, you will need to burn the photo or parchment and collect the ashes, which you will then mix with the ashes of the plants and resins.

True Witnesses

They are necessarily considered to be more powerful. They act directly from the physical plane, since they carry the vital energy of the person concerned, or the witch or wizard. They represent the magical fluid and the very essence of a being or person. Their power is believed to be almost immediate. True witnesses include nails, hair, saliva, blood, semen, and other bodily fluids. They can also be tears mixed with ink, for example to obtain more precise messages (from the deceased being mourned) or to get an answer concerning a loved one (if the tears were shed for them). In all cases, the real witnesses will be added to your ink bottle as they are, without being burned. And even if this choice of ingredients (hair, blood, nails, etc.) seems strange or frightening to most people, they are essential substances for many witches and wizards in many esoteric traditions around the world.

Other types of evidence that are essential in many magical acts include symbols, sigils, and magical seals. These should not be confused with paper on which a name and surname or ordinary symbols are written.

The magical signatures represented by symbols (such as bind runes, sigils, or magical seals) allow energies to be directed and channeled in a very powerful way. To use them as ingredients and witnesses in your magical ink, simply draw them on paper, charge them, enchant them using a ritual, and then burn them before mixing them with the rest of the powdered ashes that will be added to your ink.

This category of witnesses also includes elements that carry vital energy of animal origin, such as snake venom, hair, feathers, fangs, nails, teeth, blood, etc. All are also recognized as powerful witnesses and used in certain magical acts, rites, or special invocations.

Essential Oils

One of the advantages of modern witchcraft is that you can add a few drops of essential oils to magical inks.

Although this is optional, essential oils help stabilize homemade inks and ensure they last longer. Depending on their symbolism, they will also accentuate your magical intentions.

Choose one essential oil per magical ink, and always base your choices on your intentions, the requirements of the ritual, and magical correspondences. The essential oils I recommend are:

- Atlas cedar
- Cypress
- Clove
- Wintergreen
- Lavender
- Ylang-ylang
- Frankincense
- Olibanum
- Rose geranium
- Palmarosa
- Ravintsara

Minerals

Just like essential oils, adding minerals to your magic ink bottles is optional. If they are among the allies you like to include in your magical preparations, here is a short list of those that are particularly suitable for making magic inks. This list only includes minerals that are easy to find.

- Rock crystal: Amplification, harmonization, and channeling of energies; protection, clairvoyance, and higher planes.
- Amethyst: Spirituality, protection, divination, mediumship, intuition, and clairvoyance. Has an influence on the parapsychological faculties as a whole.
- Smoky quartz: Divination, grounding, travel, and connection to subtle planes.
- Rose quartz: Love, romance. Everything related to emotional healing and sensitivity.
- Green aventurine: Luck, prosperity, good fortune, and travel.
- Carnelian: Vital energy, sexual energy, and energy flow.
- Garnet: Passion, love, sexuality, and vitality.

- Obsidian: Protection, witchcraft, grounding, enchantment, defensive magic, and protection against the evil eye.
- Tourmaline: Protection (especially psychic) and grounding.
- Sunstone: Vitality, warmth, optimism, happiness, abundance, and sun protection.
- Emerald Beryl: Stone of knowledge also used in witchcraft for love magic. Strong bonds, harmony, blessing of unions, marriage, fertility, wisdom, happiness, and connection with the subtle bodies.
- The different moonstones including rainbow moonstone, black moonstone, peach, green (garnierite), or blue (belomorite): Intuition, moon rituals, psychic gifts, gentleness, clairvoyance, dreams, and divination arts.

CONSECRATING YOUR INKS THROUGH RITUAL

Consecration through ritual consists of imbuing an object with energy and magical intent by blessing it and giving it a role in esoteric practice.

The object, ink, and magical preparation that are ritually consecrated thereby assume a sacred rather than profane dimension.

This is why all tools and ingredients in witchcraft are systematically consecrated.

There are several ways to imbue your tools with such energetic and magical power, but when it comes to plants and resins, I recommend consecrating them before reducing them to ash.

The Magic Circle

The purpose of the magic circle is to protect, concentrate, and contain within a specific space the energy and magic that will be created, amplified, and projected there. Whichever method you choose, you will need to clean and purify your space beforehand, both physically and energetically. It is important to point out that this circle is actually a sphere, a bubble, a magical and sacred space that you need to visualize in three dimensions. A magic circle can be large if the ritual requires you to stand inside it, or small if, for example, you are performing a magical preparation on your altar. Whether the sorcerer or the witch is inside or outside, as a general rule they will face north, the direction that corresponds to the element Earth.

There are different techniques for projecting your magic circle. It can be simple or more complex. It can be made with salt, chalk, or through visualization. Allies can be added, such as minerals or tarot cards. However, you must always be consistent in your choice of stones and tools. In some practices, especially when projected outdoors, it can be made of stones, flowers, branches, and so forth.

Traditionally, the circle is drawn with salt, as it optimizes protection and purifies, protects, sanctifies, wards off evil, and embodies the Earth element.

When you have good control over your own energy, you can also project your magic circle through visualization and/or with an athame, your magic wand, or even with your fingers (either the index finger or the index and middle fingers).

The circle is drawn starting from the east, the cardinal point of the rising sun, moving clockwise (east, south, west, north). Once you return to the east, the circle is complete. When your ritual is finished, you can open your circle by following the same steps in reverse.

You can make the classic circle, but you can also add a pentacle (often used to amplify energies and protection) or white candles at the points representing the tips of the pentagram. On a simple circle, place candles at the four cardinal points, each representing an element (see correspondences below*). During these different steps, you can use magic ink to supplement them (for example, to draw the circle or to draw or coat the symbols used in the ritual).

Correspondences related to the magic circle

Direction	Element	Color(s)	Traditional tool
North	Earth	Green, brown, or black	Salt or earth
East	Air	Yellow, white, gray, or black	Incense
South	Fire	Red or dark orange	Another candle (of a different color)
West	Water	Blue	Chalice or cauldron

There are many objects and symbols that can represent the four elements and find a place in your magic circle depending on your desires, needs, and beliefs.

*For example, you can choose colored candles according to the correspondences and engrave the alchemical symbol corresponding to the element where it will be placed.

In summary:

1. Open your magic circle by drawing it starting from the east.
2. Place your ritual incense in the east (air element), a candle in a color that corresponds to your ritual (or a white candle if you don't have one) in the south (fire element), and the chalice filled with water (or your cauldron if you don't have one) in the west (water element). To the north (earth element), place the bowl filled with salt (or earth).
3. Recite your formula (here is an example):

With this incense, I consecrate this circle.
With the sacred fire, I consecrate this circle.
With the water from this chalice, I consecrate this circle.
With the salt of the earth, I consecrate this circle.

(For each sentence, turn yourself to face the corresponding cardinal point.)

Your circle is now ready, and you can begin. If your ritual requires you to stand inside the circle, then you must not leave it until the ritual is complete.

Ritual Consecration

Here is a simple method for consecrating your magical ink once it has been created.

1. Project your magic circle: It can be physical (salt, candles, etc.) or not. It can be represented on your altar, which is a

bubble of sacred energy for its sorcerer, or on the ground.

2. Place your ink bottle in the center.
3. Use visualization and your natural magnetism to channel your energies. Focus your intentions on your ink bottle. If possible, hold it in both hands or place your hands above the bottle. You infuse it with energy during this important step. You can also blow on the ink bottle at this point to transfer the power to it. This may be the moment when you formulate the role you are giving it as a tool. Your hands may start feeling warm or have a slight tingling sensation at this point, but you should continue the consecration until this sensation stops.
4. Call upon the elements and/or guardians or deities using the invocation or magic formula (examples are given below).
5. Give thanks. This can be done verbally and/or with offerings.

The following is an example of a formula for a classic consecration and general use in magical practice:

By the powers of the four elements.
Receive the blessing of the Earth element, the Air element, the Water element, the Fire element.
Now acquire the consecration that allows me to obtain the perfect result of my will from you.
So may it be.

For my red ink intended for work related to love, passion, and sexuality, I use red myrrh and acacia resin ashes mixed with rose, jasmine, and lemon balm ashes. In general, I use the blessing of a goddess associated with love to ritualize my ink. Here is an example with Aphrodite.

O Aphrodite, goddess of love and sensuality,
May your blessings be spread,
With every drop of this sacred ink.

You can do the same for each ink of different colors and intentions that you can link to a corresponding deity.

Once your ink has been ritualized, it becomes operational and blessed for your magical practice. If I had to add one last little extra element, I would advise you to "label" your inks by associating them with a symbol or sigil (a magical signature). Old ink bottles are often engraved and difficult to label. One solution is to stick your label underneath the container.

SOME TRADITIONAL BLENDS TO INSPIRE YOU

In the following section, I am going to give you recipes for some "tried and tested" blends. Some are traditional mixtures from certain esoteric traditions like Hoodoo, High magic, and older traditions. Others come from the synergies of combined plants and resins that I use personally.

A few of these mixtures have names that come from Hoodoo or Hermetic traditions. Because ink serves as a magical analogy for blood (see p. 6), the names of several of these recipes begin with the words "Blood of . . ." I have retained this witchcraft tradition in naming my personal recipes.

I list the traditional ingredients, but also effective variations that can serve the same purposes. For the proportions, you can use equal parts of each ingredient.

Dove's Blood Ink

This is the name given to the ink used to write or perform spells related to love, passion, and relationships in Hoodoo magic. It is also the ink of choice for anyone who wants to write down their wishes and help them come true. Often made from red ink, it can also be made from black ink.

The traditional ingredients used for this ink are rose, laurel, cinnamon, acacia resin (or gum arabic), and dragon's blood resin.

There are many possible variations for the same purposes. Earlier in this book I listed the ingredients I use for love in general. You can therefore make the following variations:

- Red myrrh resin, acacia resin, jasmine, rose, and lemon balm
- Acacia resin, olibanum resin, hibiscus, verbena, rose, jasmine, and basil

If you are missing an ingredient, use the general magical analogies or those suggested earlier as well as your own magical correspondences.

Dove's Eye Ink

This also refers to an ink with a gentle energy in Hoodoo magic. It is generally intended to invoke gentleness, peace, and harmony in general. It can be used for celebrations, spells calling for joy and happiness, rituals for peace of mind, or to invoke positive energies. It will also be made with a red or black base.

The traditional ingredients used are vanilla, cardamom, marjoram, red carnation, red talc, and frankincense resin.

Tree Ink or Ink from the Blood of the Ancestors

Tree ink is a bit like the "DIY" ink of inks. It is particularly useful for drawing magical symbols. All you need is a simple piece of wood or twig (preferably from a sacred tree such as oak, apple, birch, chestnut, beech, fir, maple, alder, or willow). Then, simply burn the end and use it to mark your surface.

Trees are symbols of wisdom. I associate them with the roots of life and ancestors. That is why I use certain ashes from the bark of sacred trees in the making of inks for rituals related to ancestors, the past, ancient roots, and karma.

I am happy to offer you this mixture, which I have named "Ancestral Blood Ink" (always with respect for tradition), which can be made with black, purple, or green ink. The ingredients are oak, birch, and beech bark (if necessary, you can substitute the bark of another sacred tree from the list), pine resin, licorice, and angelica root.

Heart Tear Ink

This ink is intended for healing work—especially emotional healing. Like the previous ink, it can be used to promote gentleness, peace, and harmony. It is created from a mixture inspired by my personal magical practice and based on red or black ink.

The ingredients used are jasmine, rose, chamomile, lavender, red myrrh resin, sandalwood, and acacia.

Dragon's Blood Ink

This ink is intended for spells of strength, martial qualities, and power. It can also be used to attract money or material abundance.

As its name suggests, it can be used for draconic magic or healing, but it is primarily a representation of additional power for any spell. It can be created using ink of your choice.

The traditional ingredients used are dragon's blood resin and acacia resin (gum arabic).

Wizards often add to this composition to strengthen it according to their needs. For example, if I want to optimize it for luck rituals, or to attract money or material abundance, I add red clover, citrus peel, and hawthorn.

To accentuate the effect of a spell, I would add gentian root and angelica root to the traditional base.

Deer Blood Ink

This is an ink that I make for all classic rituals and spells related to protection. It is made from black ink and will be useful for the protection ritual described later on page 88.

The ingredients used are lavender, cedar, sage, olibanum, benzoin, copal, and sandalwood resins.

Bat Blood Ink

This is the name given to the ink of discord in Hoodoo magic. It is made to cast spells that sow dissent and quarrels. It is also used in certain magical pacts, to bind or curse, to cast the evil eye, and for spells and possessions. It is made from black or red ink.

The traditional ingredients used are dragon's blood resin, myrrh resin, acacia resin (or gum arabic), and cinnamon.

Jupiter Ink

This ink is used in rituals for success, prosperity, and growth on the psychic and material planes. Ideally, it should be made with black ink.

The traditional ingredients used are bergamot, nutmeg, and acacia resin (gum arabic).

Neptune Ink

This is the ink I use for all spells or rituals that concern dreams or the dream world in general, prophetic visions, and various divination practices. It can be made with black, purple, or blue ink.

The ingredients are myrrh resin (or camphor resin as a substitute); acacia resin, wormwood, mugwort, cloves, and bird cherry.

Pact Ink

In the occult world, this ink is so named because it is used for pacts or agreements made with entities (especially negative ones) or with demons. The traditional composition of this ink can be found in the *Grimorium Verum*, an occult work from the sixteenth century published by Alibeck the Egyptian. I am sharing this recipe with you for your personal knowledge and because I want to cover everything there is to know about magical inks. However, I do not encourage you to make it or attempt any rituals involving it. It is usually made with black ink as a base.

The traditional ingredients used are badamier nuts (*Terminalia catappa*), acacia resin (gum arabic), copper sulfate, or Roman vitriol (a mineral associated with Melanterite), which can be found in Hoodoo and botanica shops. Be careful, as these are dangerous, corrosive substances that are deadly to humans. They must not be ingested under any circumstances. Handle with care!

There are variations—not necessarily less dangerous—with ingredients by country witches, including acacia resin (gum arabic), dried fly agaric mushrooms, and black henbane. Fresh belladonna berries are squeezed to extract the juice, which is added to the ink. But be careful, as these plants are "poisonous ladies" that can cause damage and are unforgiving if mishandled or misused. The potency of belladonna berries and the juice that can be extracted from them is enough to make them both a powerful and dangerous poison and magical ink.

Devil's Tears Ink

I imagine that the previous ink may be a little frightening given the use it's intended for. I now give you an ink that I have called "Devil's Tears Ink," which could also be called "Evil Tears Ink" to remain with the classic names for inks. This synergy of plants and resins is offered to you this time to counter, exorcise, or banish negative entities; or even to break an agreement or pact made with them or with a demon. It is also created on a black ink base and can be used for any form of counter-spell.

The ingredients used are olibanum resin, myrrh, benzoin, and storax (the ingredients of pontifical incense) in equal parts, camphor resin, St. John's wort, sage, alchemilla (lady's mantle), sulfur, and dried elderberries.

Cat's Blood Ink

Created from black ink, this ink will be helpful for you when casting spells against psychic and energetic attacks, and for classic banishing rituals such as the one suggested on page 94, or to break toxic ties with a person.

The ingredients used are: asafoetida, elderberry, St. John's wort, acacia resin (gum arabic), and frankincense.

Zephyr Ink

For a wind that brings renewal, this ink is intended for all rituals that call for change, new beginnings, rebirth, or a turning point in one's life. It is concocted on a base of black or blue ink. It can be used for the renewal spell on page 97.

The ingredients used are sage, mint, hawthorn, star anise, acacia resin (gum arabic), and dammar gum.

Wolf's Blood Ink

This is the mixture I consecrate for rituals of fertility, fecundity, and prosperity. Used with Zephyr ink, it celebrates the spring season. It can be made using ink of any color you like.

The ingredients used are sesame seeds, ginger, grape seeds, apple seeds, olibanum resin, and acacia resin (gum arabic).

Four

Using Magical Inks

CREATING MAGIC SPELLS

The primary and most common use of inks is for drawing and writing.

Inks allow us to leave marks on different media, to record a specific moment of life and history. Ultimately, they allow us to immortalize what they are recording through their graphic representations.

Ink allows sacred words to be transcribed into sacred writing. In the esoteric world, magical inks are used in the same way:

- To write a grimoire, and more specifically to collect prayers, magic spells, or invocations
- To draw symbols, sigils, and seals
- To write magic words or intentions during rituals
- To create objects, talismans, or amulets

Essentially, all spells, rituals, or creations that require a written record or the drawing of a symbol may include the use of magical inks.

Beyond those uses, magical inks can be particularly helpful allies in certain defensive magic practices, as well as in several types of spells such as protection, enchantments and disenchantments, counter-spells, breaking toxic bonds, and so forth. This gives me the opportunity to share with you some of my creations, spells, and rituals.

A FEW TIPS FOR CREATING YOUR OWN MAGIC SPELLS

Words have been considered sacred since ancient times. Magic spells and incantations are part of most rituals. The magic of sound is a form of magic in its own right. Sound created through the voice sets energies in motion. The words chosen to express the will to act allow you to direct your energies to achieve the magical objective. There are nuances that distinguish magic spells, prayers, and invocations from each other, but they all share in common the establishment of a magical connection and the projection of a wish or intention. Often in the stages of a ritual, powers are conferred through the spell.

Whether recited, sung, or chanted, magic formulas help bridge the gap between your conscious and unconscious mind, and the subtle worlds. By creating your own spell, you are already creating an intention and a magical action.

The number 3 is associated with creation, which explains why it is often recommended to recite formulas three times (or over and over) and to use these phrases only in the context of your rituals.

Rhymes often help to give rhythm to your speech. Summarize clearly the situation you want to achieve, avoiding negations. The phrase should resonate with you, like a mantra. It can sometimes even put you into a trancelike state. Express it with faith, respecting the energies you are addressing. Avoid stammering and be confident. You can create a phrase or formula for each of your creations or for each ritual they are intended for.

SALT AND INK SPELLS

Here is a method for making your own salts. These can be used to draw a magic circle or as ingredients in your amulets, talismans, charms, and spells.*

Salt is an element that purifies, protects, sanctifies, wards off evil, and symbolizes the Earth element. It remains one of the most effective magical tools available to us from Mother Nature. These salts will also be very useful for performing some of the spells I suggest below.

You should realize that when ink and salt are mixed, the color may vary. I have observed that salt often turns blue when mixed with red or purple ink purchased from stores. This is not a problem in itself, as the chemical reaction does not alter the intentions or powers of the ink once it has become magical ink, even if the salt doesn't necessarily take on the "color" of the magical act or intention. Depending on your needs and intentions, you can not only create colored magical ink and mix it with salt but also add ingredients to amplify its powers in your magical practice. The salts offered here can be used alone

*Such as in bottles, sachets, offerings, celebrations, and other magical preparations.

as a spell or a charm in its own right, and not just as a magical tool. Placed in a vial or pouch, they can be placed anywhere to protect your home (with protective salt), to attract good luck (with abundance salt), and so on. Give thought to how you want to consecrate your tools and materials beforehand.

The method is similar for each salt. Here we will look at:

- Black protective salt (the one that is used most often), made with black magic ink
- An example of how to make red salt for rituals related to love, using red ink, of course
- Salt for everything related to divination, using purple ink
- Salt dedicated to abundance, using green ink

Black Protective Salt

Ingredients

- Your black magic ink (such as deer blood ink, for example, p. 63)
- White salt
- A mortar
- A container (such as a soup bowl or a salad bowl)
- Black pepper
- A small piece of parchment on which you will write your magic formula or your intention; for example, "protection against negative energies" accompanied by a sigil, a seal, or a protective symbol such as a pentacle or a rune such as Algiz ᛉ
- Something to burn the plants, resins, and parchment (i.e., matches, charcoal, and a cauldron or suitable container)
- A glass vial to store your protective salt once it has been created

- Your dried plants (choose at least three different ones from the following list and adjust the quantities according to the size of your storage container) sage, lavender, cedar, juniper berries, asafoetida, nettle, mugwort, rosemary, star anise, burdock
- One or two natural incense resins from the following: frankincense, benzoin, myrrh, or acacia
- A white candle and incense to burn during your ritual
- Optional: eggshells if you use them in your defensive and protective magic

Preparation

Burn the roots, resins, and parchment (after writing your spell on it), then collect the cooled ashes in your container.

In your mortar, grind the peppercorns and eggshell (if using) into a fine powder and add it to the ashes.

Place the salt in your container and pour a few drops of magic ink over it (adjust according to the amount of salt; there is no need to color it heavily), then mix well.

Add your fine powder and mix until you have a smooth consistency.

Ritual

Cast your magic circle and light the incense and candle.

Place your container in the center of the circle.

Place your hands on either side of the container,

breathe calmly, and focus your energy and intentions through your hands. You should feel them getting warmer.

When you feel ready, recite your spell or invocation:

By the powers of the four elements.
Receive the blessing
of the element Earth, of the element Air,
of the element Water, of the element Fire.
Now acquire the consecration
that allows me to obtain from you
the perfect result of my will.
For protection and defense
against evil, you will be devoted to me.

Store your salt in the vial intended for it; it is now ready for use. As with any bottled magical preparation, you may label it with a sigil or symbol.

Red Salt of Love and Attraction

Ingredients

- Your red magic ink (dove's blood, p. 61, for example)
- Pink Himalayan salt or white salt
- A mortar
- A container (such as a soup bowl or a salad bowl)

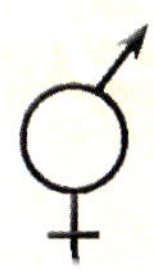

- A small piece of parchment on which you have written your magic spell or intention (e.g., "love," "harmony," "blessing") and a sigil, seal, or symbol related to love (see example opposite)
- Something to burn the plants, resins, and parchment (i.e., matches, charcoal, and a cauldron or suitable container)
- A glass vial to store your protective salt once it has been created

- Your dried plants (choose at least three different ones from the following list and adjust the quantities according to the size of your storage container): rose, jasmine, verbena, basil, hibiscus, cinnamon, lavender, ginger, ginseng
- One or two natural incense resins from the following: myrrh, acacia, pine, sandalwood, dammar gum
- A pink or red candle and incense to burn during your ritual

Preparation

Burn your roots, resins, and parchment (after writing the formula on it), then collect the cooled ashes in your container.

You can also burn the plants at the same time, but for this salt, you can just grind them into a powder and store them without burning them. Then all you have to do is add them to your preparation when needed.

In your mortar, grind the ashes into a fine powder.

Add the salt to your container along with a few drops of magic ink (adjust according to the amount of salt; there is no need to color it too much). Mix well.

Then add your ashes (and dried plants reduced to powder) and mix again to obtain a homogeneous substance.

Ritual

Cast your magic circle and light the incense and candle.

Place your container in the center of the circle.

Place your hands on either side of the container, breathing calmly and focusing your energy and intentions through your hands. You should feel them getting warmer.

When you feel ready, recite your formula or invocation.

By the powers of the four elements.
Receive the blessing of the Earth element, the Air element,
the Water element, and the Fire element.
Now acquire the consecration
that allows me to obtain from you
the perfect result of my will.
You will be devoted to my magic.

Store your salt in the vial intended for it as it is now ready for use. When you put a magical preparation in a container, you can draw a sigil or symbol on the label.

Purple Divination Salt

Ingredients

- Your purple magic ink
- White salt
- A mortar
- A container (such as a basin or salad bowl)
- A small piece of parchment on which you have written your magic spell or intention of protection, intuition, and clairvoyance; and a sigil, seal, or symbol of divination (such as an eye, for example)

- Something to burn the plants, resins, and parchment (i.e., matches, charcoal, and a cauldron or suitable container)
- A glass vial to store your protective salt once it has been created
- Your dried plants (choose at least three different ones from the following list and adjust the

quantities according to the size of your storage container): absinthe, lavender, sage, mugwort, jasmine, angelica, star anise, burdock, valerian, cloves

- One or two natural incense resins from the following: camphor, olibanum, storax, sandalwood, benzoin, copal
- A purple candle and incense to burn during your ritual

Preparation

Burn your roots, resins, and parchment (after writing the formula on it), then collect the cooled ashes in your container.

In your mortar, grind the ashes into a fine powder.

Add the salt to your container along with a few drops of magic ink (adjust according to the amount of salt; there is no need to give it a deep color). Mix well.

Then add your ashes and mix until you have a smooth consistency.

Ritual

Cast your magic circle and light the incense and candle.

Place your container in the center of the circle.

Place your hands on either side of the container, breathing calmly and focusing your energy and intentions through your hands. You should feel them start to get warm.

When you feel ready, recite your formula or invocation.

By the powers of the four elements.
Receive the blessing of the element Earth, the element Air,
the element Water, the element Fire.
Now acquire the consecration
that allows me to obtain from you
the perfect result of my will.
You will be devoted to my magic.

Store your salt in the vial intended for it. It is now ready for use. As with any bottled magical preparation, you can label it with a sigil or symbol.

Green Salt of Abundance

Ingredients

- Your green magic ink
- White salt
- A mortar
- A container (such as a soup bowl or a salad bowl)
- A small piece of parchment on which you have written your magic formula or intention (for example: "abundance, luck, and material prosperity") and a sigil, seal, or divination symbol (such as the Ankh cross and the rune seal shown here)

- Something to burn the plants, resins, and parchment (i.e., matches, charcoal, and a cauldron or suitable container)
- A glass vial to store your protective salt once it has been created
- Your dried plants (choose at least three different ones from the following list and adjust the

quantities according to the size of your storage container): burdock, lemon balm, cedar, mint, hawthorn, citrus, clover, cinnamon, sesame seeds, mustard seeds, grape seeds, apple seeds

- One or two natural incense resins from the following: frankincense, pine, acacia, sandalwood, benzoin, copal
- A green candle and incense to burn during your ritual

Preparation

Burn your roots, resins, and parchment (after writing the spell on it), then collect the cooled ashes in your container.

In your mortar, grind the ashes into a fine powder.

Place the salt in your bowl and add a few drops of magic ink (adjust according to the amount of salt you have; there is no need to color the salt too much), then mix well.

Next, add your ashes and mix until you have a smooth consistency.

Ritual

Cast your magic circle and light the incense and candle.

Place your container in the center of the circle.

Place your hands on either side of the container, breathing calmly and focusing your energy and intentions through your hands. You should feel them getting warm.

When you feel ready, recite your formula or invocation.

By the powers of the four elements.
Receive the blessing of the element Earth, the element Air,
the element Water, the element Fire.
Now acquire the consecration
that allows me to obtain from you
the perfect result of my will.
You will be devoted to my magic.

Store your salt in the vial intended for it. It is now ready for use. As with any bottled magical preparation, you can label it with a sigil or symbol.

RITUALS, SPELLS, AND COUNTER-SPELLS

For performing this kind of magic using magical inks, you will need to use, as in all rituals, material that has been consecrated and to do the operation inside a circle.

You can also adapt the color of the candles to match the intention on which the ritual is based as well as create an anointing oil that specifically relates to these candles and the spell's intention.

The symbols used are only there by way of suggestion, founded on your own magical correspondences and beliefs.

Counter-Spells

These are defensive magic rituals that consist of countering the effects of a spell and nullifying its effectiveness as much as possible (see, for example, the ritual for breaking a spell on p. 91) or even returning it to the sender.

There are several types of counter-spells, and, in my opinion, they are among the most complicated spells, primarily because they most often require effective and rapid results. Indeed, when we call upon the resources of defensive magic, it is often because our own energy shield and psychic strength have not been strong enough to defend us, because protective rituals could not be put in place in time, or were proved to be ineffective. This requires moving to the next level and appealing to higher forces.

Defensive magic is used to counter a very wide range of magic. In particular, we may have to fight against:

- Classic energy or psychic attacks (the evil eye, bewitchment, etc.)
- Being affected by spiritually impure and negative vibrations emitted by a place or a person, consciously or unconsciously
- Curses, possessions, or struggles against entities or demons (in short, what is known as pure and simple black magic)

I won't go into the many techniques for countering spells (perhaps one day I'll have the opportunity to devote an entire book to them). I'll simply offer you a few defensive magic rituals in which ink is a powerful ally.

Allow me to offer a word of advice: If you are new to esoteric practices and have the opportunity to seek help, don't attempt your first rituals alone. Even experienced practitioners often seek the assistance of a colleague. The rituals I suggest here can be performed entirely on your own. Their simple protocol will safely guide your magic. However, they may not be sufficient to combat black magic emanating from very powerful forces or to break a powerful curse.

In a way, counter-spells represent the clash of opposing forces, the collision of two distinct types of magic, a duel between two sorcerers. A magical confrontation that should not be taken lightly!

In the case of counter-spells and spell-breaking, there are often two types of situations:

- You know where the evil spell comes from or who cast it.
- You have no idea, or at least no certainty.

The "easiest" spells and curses to break are those whose source (the spell caster) is known, or where there is a material trace or tangible evidence shedding light on how they were cast. This could be, for example, a written note, a dagger, the bottle containing the spell, or a tool used during the ritual.

If you are certain of the identity of the person who cast the spell on you, you can use a physical item belonging to them to counter it: hair, nails, any bodily fluid (blood, semen, saliva, etc.). If you have no physical "evidence," use a photo with their first and last name and date of birth. As a last resort, write down whatever information you have on a piece of parchment.

In any case, you start with a clear advantage because you know who to direct your defensive magic against. If you are not certain, you will have to proceed differently.

In all cases, the purification and protection of the victim of the spell must be reinforced. According to various beliefs, there are several ways to do this: prayer, a purifying bath with salt or lead, meditation, the use of black water or ink in a protective spell such as the one suggested on page 88.

All spiritual or esoteric methods focused on the victim of the spell are worth trying. And when you don't know where the energy or magic attack is coming from, these are the most common remedies.

Ritual of Protection

Here is a magic procedure that includes the use of magical ink. It offers protection by strengthening the individual's energy shield. By cleansing the aura of negative energies it helps to purify it.

Tools and ingredients

- Your magical ink; black is the most appropriate color for protection (see examples of inks, such as deer blood ink on p. 63).
- Some hair, nails, or a little blood from the person you want to protect or counteract
- If none of these are available, a photo of your "target" with their first and last name and, if possible, their birth date written on the back. The target can be the person you want to protect (in the case of a protection ritual) or the person you want to counteract (as in the case of a banishing ritual).
- If you are unable to print a photo or do not have one available, simply write the person's first and last name on a piece of paper with your magic ink. You can also add a drawn symbol, such as the

Algiz rune (see p. 133), but you can create your own symbol, seal, or sigil.

- Your protective salt (see p. 70)
- A black candle preferably (if unavailable use a white one), on which you can also carve the chosen symbol, and then spread magic ink over it using your finger
- Incense: You can use simple resins or create specific ones, as in our case for energy protection

Implementing the ritual

Light the incense and candle.

Draw your magic circle using the salt provided for this purpose (see p. 70) and place your witness in the center (photos, hair, and so on).

Place your hands over the photo, concentrating your energy and intention, and recite your formula or prayer. Here is an example:

O goddess Hecate, protector of witches, protect and bless
(name of the person), drive away the harmful energies from their life,
may light triumph over the darkness that surrounds them.

Take your candle and pour a few drops of wax into the circle (around the photo) to seal your spell. Then put it back and let it burn down completely.

Once your candle has fully burned down, the ritual is complete. Ideally, bury the remains of the ritual (salt + photo), or burn the photo in the center of the circle (in your cauldron), dilute everything in water, and pour it down the sink.

Lastly, I recommend leaving an offering of your choice as a thank-you to the goddess or energy you called upon during your ritual.

Breaking a Spell

Breaking a spell is part of the defensive magic common to all esoteric traditions. The methods may differ, but the objective remains the same: to break the spell and undo it, thereby causing its negative energy to vanish. To do this, we will look at one possible method using magic ink. The salt used symbolizes purification and protection against evil spells, and dissolving the writing in moon water or holy water will wash away negative energies and break the spell. In addition, water is both a mirror and a gateway to the subtle planes. It is on the astral plane that most energy attacks and spells used to counter them take place.

Materials

- A black or white candle (which you can coat with magic oil and engrave with a symbol, see example symbol for banishment on p. 136)
- Your black magic ink, preferably soluble (such as dragon's blood, p. 63)
- A container (such as a bowl)
- Holy spring water, moon water, or cold water

- Salt. Depending on the objective, choose from the salts listed on page 70. Black salt is suitable for everything, but if you want to break a spell or a love spell, use red salt.
- Natural incense made from resins and plants (refer to the correspondences on page 41 and 44. Here is an example of a suitable combination: frankincense resin, storax resin, lavender, mugwort, and cedar.
- Parchment. If you know what spell has been cast or have a written record of it, write down what needs to be undone or which spell needs to be broken. In the case of a curse or the evil eye cast on you, you can simply write: "Here is the mark of the curse." It does not matter if you know the origin of the occult attack. If, as is often the case, you have no information, you can simply use your magic ink to draw a sigil, seal, or symbol on your parchment (for example, a simple eye or the Eye of Horus, or the witch's rune called the Sickle or the bind runes listed on p. 136 for the banishing ritual). In both cases, write the date of your ritual to anchor your intention in space-time.

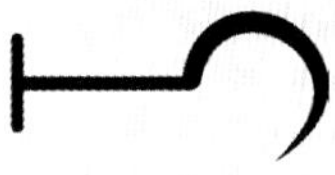

Performing the ritual

Light the incense and candle and open your magic circle.

With your ink, draw a protective symbol on your wrists (for example, the rune Algiz).

Place your container in the center of the circle.

Put the unfolded parchment in the container.

Throw a small handful of your salt on the parchment while saying these words: "By this sacred and purifying salt, I cast out evil."

Then add the holy water while reciting your formula, prayer, or invocation. For example: "By the protective magic and divine light, the spell is broken (say your first and last name or those of the person under the spell) is now free."

Once the ink on the parchment begins to fade, the counter-spell is working.

Once the ritual is complete and the candle has burned out, throw the contents of the container into the toilet. Important information: Do not burn the parchment. In witchcraft, burning is used to activate a spell, but here, the goal is not to reactivate the evil spell, but to dissolve it. Instead, allow the paper to disintegrate as much as possible in the purifying water, even if this requires a little patience.

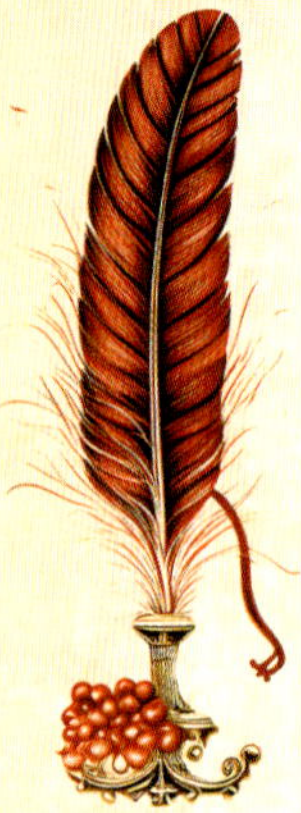

Banishing Ritual

This ritual makes it possible to banish the negative energies, intentions, or effects of an evil spell. It also forms part of a disenchantment protocol, given the fact it permits you to construct a barrier against a spell that someone may cast against you. In any case, here is the basic framework for first performing the banishment ritual, then after, using this same framework, to perform a ritual to make space for renewal.

Tools and ingredients

- A plate or dish in which you can put about 1 to 3 cm of spring water, moon water, or Florida water
- Your magic ink (black is the most appropriate color for banishing)
- An item belonging to or representing your target (the person you want to counter, as in this banishing ritual), such as a few hairs, nails, or a little of their blood
- If none of these things are available, a photo of them with their first and last name and date of birth (if you know it) written on the back. If you are unable to find or print a photo, a simple piece of paper or

parchment on which you write their first and last names and draw a symbol such as the bind runes I use for this ritual (p. 136) or a seal or sigil of your own invention. A dictionary of symbols can give you some suitable ideas.

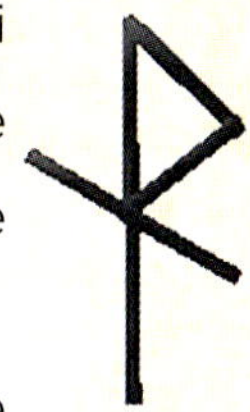

- A mixture of mugwort, pepper, and/or chili powder ground with a pestle, and white or black salt. You can use black salt like the one suggested on page 72.
- A black candle (or white if you don't have one) on which you can carve the symbol you have chosen and spread magic ink over it using your finger
- Incense: You can use simple resins or create a specific one, as in the example I've given here for banishing negative energies

Performing the ritual

To perform a banishing ritual, it is best to do so during the waning moon.

Prepare your mixture of plants and salt to be ground into a powder with a pestle. The salt must be black, preferably the one suggested on page 72.

Place your plate filled with water in the center of your magic circle and light your candle and incense.

Place the representative item (hair, nails, blood, photo, or parchment) on the water in the center of the plate.

Pour your mixture of herbs and salt over it.

Add the magic ink until it covers the photo or parchment.

Place your hands over the plate, focusing your energy and intention, and recite your spell. You can choose your own phrase, prayer, or invocation according to your needs, beliefs, or the energies you prefer to work with. Otherwise, here is what I suggest:

> *O goddess Hecate, protector of witches, banish from my life the*
> *negative energies and evil intentions of (name of the person).*
> *May my strength and will triumph over theirs.*

Take the candle and pour a few drops of wax onto the plate to seal your spell. Set it aside and let it burn down completely.

Once your candle has burned out, throw the entire contents of the plate into the toilet and flush.

Finally, I recommend that you leave an offering of your choice as a token of gratitude to the goddess or energy you have called upon for your ritual. If you feel you need to repeat the ritual, don't hesitate to do so.

Ritual to Clear a Space so Renewal Can Occur

The procedure is the same as the one used for the banishing ritual. You can use this method to dispel the energies that make it impossible for you to clear the space necessary for something new to arise in your life, or, for example, to free yourself of an addiction or other dependency.

Ingredients

- Instead of a photograph, use a piece of parchment on which you write exactly what you want to get rid of and use some of your hair, a little of your blood or your nails
- A white or green candle
- A mixture of sage, mint, and hawthorn powder, and abundance salt (see p. 81) or a mixture suited to your personal magical correspondences and intentions, based on the advice given above
- A symbol associated with renewal, such as the Ehwaz rune ᛖ or your own seal or sigil creation

Ritual

Place your plate filled with water in the center of your magic circle.

Light your candle and incense.

In the center of the plate of water, dip the parchment indicating your wish, then your hair (or nails or blood), and pour your mixture of herbs and salt over it.

Add the magic ink until the ink entirely covers the parchment.

Place your hands over the plate, focusing your energy and intention, and recite the formula according to your wishes and beliefs. For example:

O Hecate, goddess of renewal,
help me to take the path that is mine,
banishing all that is inappropriate.

Take the candle and pour a few drops of wax onto the plate to seal your fate. Then place it back on the candle holder and let it burn down completely.

Once your candle has gone out, throw the entire contents of the plate into the toilet and flush. Finish with an offering of thanks.

Luck Spell

This is a spell to attract good luck. You will have to perform it in a magic circle and your materials need to be consecrated. The luck spell is best performed on a Thursday, Jupiter's day, and/or during a waxing or full moon.

Materials

- Your magic ink (see suggestions on p. 11)
- A green candle (which can be coated with magic oil and engraved with a symbol)
- A medium-sized piece of parchment (large enough to be folded) on which you will write your intentions (for example, "I wish to attract good luck into my life"), then draw your seal or a symbol related to prosperity (such as the runic seal, see photo p. 136) and write your intentions

Ritual

Place the parchment in your magic circle and light your candle.

Place your hands over the parchment and concentrate fully on your intention as you recite the formula. Here is an example of a formula for good luck:

O Njörd, god of the sea and winds,
bring me good fortune.
I welcome your blessings and thank you.

Then fold the parchment by bringing the corners toward the center and seal it with the wax from the candle.

Let the candle burn out completely, then make an offering to your deity or give thanks for the energy you have requested.

Keep your parchment in your wallet or in a pocket of your purse.

Love Spell

This procedure is the same as the one used for the luck spell. It should preferably be done on a Friday, the day of Venus, and/or during a waxing moon or full moon.

Materials

- Your magic ink
- A red or pink candle (which can be coated with magic oil and engraved with a symbol)
- A medium-sized piece of parchment (large enough to be folded) on which you will write your intentions with your magic ink (for example, "I wish to attract sincere and gracious love into my life"), then draw your seal or a symbol related to love (such as the bind rune shown below).

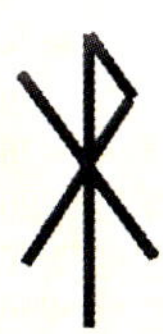

Ritual

Place the parchment in your magic circle and light your candle.

Place your hands over the parchment and focus on your intention as you recite the magic spell for love. I suggest:

O Aphrodite, goddess of love and sensuality,
may your blessings be sent to me.

Then fold the parchment by bringing the edges toward the center and seal it with the wax from the candle.

Let the candle burn out completely, then make an offering to your deity or give thanks for the energy you have requested.

Keep your parchment under your pillow.

MAGICAL CREATIONS

Throughout all history, humans have used cosmetics. In antiquity, makeup was often made from plant and mineral ingredients. It is possible to create your own eye shadow, eyeliner, and kohl and give them magical properties. All you have to do is adapt your spell to match your intentions. These creations are inspired by ancient makeup recipes using the magic of ink to enhance their power to seduce.

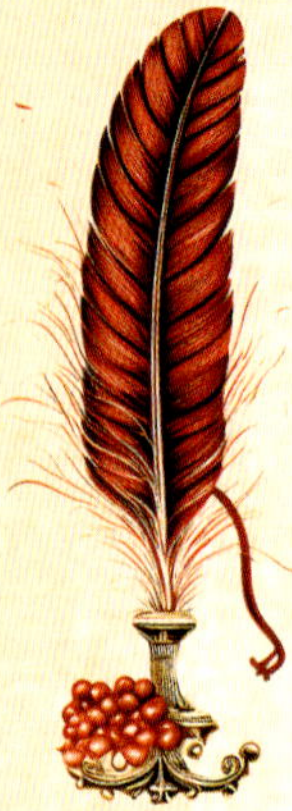

Eye Shadow

It is difficult in our day to create homemade mineral-based pigments as was possible in ancient times, with lapis lazuli, for example. This is the reason I suggest using mica to create your own eye shadow in the color you want. Mica is a mineral pigment that comes in many colors and is easy to find in stores.

Ingredients

- Mica powder in the color of your choice
- A vegetable oil such as jojoba or sweet almond
- A red or pink candle, but a white one will do if you don't have one
- Incense, see correspondences on pages 41–44
- Optional: rice powder. Often used in cosmetics throughout history and in different cultures, it is easy to find in stores. Rice has interesting symbolic powers in witchcraft, such as protection and abundance.
- A bowl to mix your ingredients
- A glass container to store your eye shadow, which can be applied with your finger or a brush

Preparation

Create your magic circle, gather your materials, and consecrate them.

Light the candle and incense, concentrate—the preparation is part of the ritual.

Place your bowl in the circle and pour in a teaspoon of mica. You can adjust the amount according to your needs or the size of the container you will use for your eyeshadow.

Optional: Add the rice powder (for 1 teaspoon of mica, use 1/4 teaspoon of rice powder).

Drip in the vegetable oil while stirring until you obtain the desired texture. You can apply some to your wrist to check that the eye shadow suits you.

Put your eye shadow in its container.

Ritual

Hold your eye shadow jar in your hands, breathe peacefully, and focus your energy and intentions through your hands. You should feel them start to get warm.

When you feel ready, recite your spell or invocation. For example, if you want your eye shadow to help you seduce, enhance your natural magnetism, make your eyes more captivating, and let magic emanate from your aura with every blink of your eyelashes, say:

O goddess Aphrodite, goddess of charm and
sensuality,
Bless what, with a blink of an eye, will transport your
magic.
Your power burns within me, my powers of
seduction are awakened,
With my magnetic aura and bewitching gaze,
I will be able to cast a spell.

Your eye shadow is now ready to use! You can use the same invocation for future creations. You can also repeat the prayer before each makeup session while looking in the mirror.

Kohl of the Goddess

Kohl, like ink, is made from plants that have been reduced to ash. You can choose a powdery or creamy texture. Here's how to easily create your own ancient goddess kohl.

Ingredients and equipment

- A container in which to store your kohl
- A vegetable oil such as olive, jojoba, or sweet almond
- A bowl
- A mortar and pestle
- Dried rose petals
- Something to burn and reduce the petals to ashes (lighter, etc.)
- Optional: an almond (unscented, untreated, and unsmoked) and tongs (charcoal tongs or tweezers, for example, so you don't burn yourself when burning the ingredients)
- Optional: mica if you want colored kohl

Preparation

Burn the petals and almond over the container with a lighter or candle.

Collect the ashes and crush them in a mortar to reduce them to as fine a powder as possible.

Add your mica (about 1/5 of the amount of ashes).

Add 2 to 3 drops of vegetable oil, depending on whether you want a powdery or creamy kohl (mix with a spoon; the mixture should not be liquid). Using a knife blade or spoon, collect the kohl and store it in the container of your choice.

Ritual

Take your kohl jar in your hands, breathe calmly, and focus your energy and intentions.

Recite your own spell or the following invocation:

O goddess Aphrodite, goddess of charm and sensuality,
Bless that which, with a blink of an eye, will transport your magic.
Your power burns within me, my powers of seduction are awakened, with my magnetic aura and bewitching gaze,
I will be able to cast a spell.

Your kohl is ready! Repeat your spell at the beginning every time you put on makeup, if you wish.

Magic Brush

It is possible to enchant all types of objects for different uses and functions. We will see how to enchant a comb or hairbrush to make them magical using a method that involves ink and magic words. The nature of the role and power conferred on the enchanted object during the ritual will depend on the ink used and the word, symbol, or seal you choose to carve on it.

Here, we will choose to enchant a brush with the intention of protection and vitality. Each time the brush passes through your hair, it will activate the magic within your aura and your physical body. To do this, we will use the runic word HLUTRAZ. *This runic word combines the magic of seven runes: Hagalaz, Laguz, Uruz, Tiwaz, Raidho, Ansuz, and Algiz.*

One important note: Traditionally, this ritual is performed with blood rather than ink, but there is nothing to stop you adding a drop of your blood to the ink. It will act as a witness to your life force, which is to be protected and amplified.

Please note that this brush or comb is not intended for everyday use, but rather as a magical tool to be used with care and with the intention of cleansing, protecting, and strengthening your vital energy. I recommend that each time you brush your hair, you reactivate the runic word by pronouncing it and making it vibrate.

For the ritual, you will need to work within a magic circle and consecrate your materials.

Materials

- A wooden brush or comb
- Your magic ink (preferably red, for vitality and the activation of positive energies)
- A knife or other tool for carving the magic word into the wood
- A fine detail paintbrush
- A red or white candle
- Incense to accompany you during your protection ritual

Ritual

Open your magic circle and place your brush or comb in the center.

Light the incense and candle.

Focus your intention in your hands and begin to carve your magic word, starting from the top and working your way down. Each time you carve a rune, say it aloud, let it resonate within you, and feel its vibration. Then move on to the next rune.

Once the word is carved, use the brush to place a single drop of ink on the first rune. This should allow the ink to soak into the wood and color your rune. Repeat the process for each rune, following the order of the word from top to bottom.

Once the word has been engraved and painted, hold the brush in both hands, look at your magic word, and say it three times. Let it resonate within you and feel its powerful vibration.

You can now end your ritual, close your magic circle, and let the candle burn out before using your brush.

Runic word, HLUTRAZ, to be engraved on the brush

THE ARTS OF DIVINATION

It appears that divination using ink stains was inspired by other methods of divination such as *oneiromancy* (divination by dreams), *hydromancy* (divination using water as a medium), and *catoptromancy* (a method of divination using the magic of mirrors). Similarly, there are similarities with *ornithomancy*, a form of divination that studies omens through the movements or songs of birds. But also with *capnomancy*, which also involves interpreting the shapes formed by smoke. Finally, there is *hematomancy*, which refers to an occult practice that uses blood magic. This was a divinatory art practiced by the Greeks, Chaldeans, Etruscans, and the inhabitants of ancient Mesopotamia.

Inkromancy

Inkromancy consists of reading the future through the ink stains made on a sheet of paper, which are then interpreted as shapes, symbols, and drawings. Each shape or drawing is a message that someone wants to convey to you. Inkromancy requires very few ingredients.

This method of divination was rigorously codified by Luce Vidi (whose real name was Angèle Vidi), a famous clairvoyant and palm reader active in the 1940s. She determined and detailed this method of divination and gave it the name inkromancy. She believed that this method shed light on the subject, their personality, their past, and also provided a wealth of information about their future. Luce Vici published the first book on inkromancy, whose title is *Les taches d'encre. Symbolisme et interprétation* (Ink Stains: Symbolism and Interpretation), in 1936 with Éditions Niclaus.

I'd like to make a little digression here, because the story is worth telling. In 1927, Georges Niclaus founded a bookshop and publishing house specializing in the occult. His niece Nicole Bussière, who succeeded him in 1964, gave her name to the publishing house, which today publishes this book on the magic of ink in France. Symbolically, as an author and occultist, this twist of fate is a huge gift from the universe. "There is no such thing as coincidence" are words I greatly agree with. They were spoken to me by the first person who laid eyes on my manuscript, Anne-Laure, the current director of Éditions Bussière and Nicole Bussière's daughter. She is a woman with an incredible aura. Chance does not exist, or let's say that it does things well.

To return to inkromancy, this method is reminiscent of a famous psychological assessment tool using ink blots known as the Rorschach test. We look at both the shapes and the drawings and observe the thoughts and feelings they evoke in us, and the familiar shapes they remind us of. The interpretation section on page 125 may help you with this. Inkromancy is a method of divination, a medium that naturally calls on your intuition and personal perceptions. As with any divination practice, two people will not necessarily see the same things. The richness and accuracy of the interpretations depend on the subtleties of the drawings and the eye observing them.

To perform divination through inkromancy, you must have everything prepared before you start. As with any divinatory art, being in the right energetic and emotional state is essential for interpreting with clarity of mind and impartiality. Some people conduct their divination sessions within a magic circle, but you can simply use incense and candles.

Materials

- A sheet of white paper (not too absorbent) in standard size (A3, A4, or US Letter)
- A pen to write on the back of the sheet
- A quill or dropper to spread your ink drops
- Black ink or ink in the color of your choice. Commercially available India ink will do the job, but I encourage you to use your own personalized ink or to ritualize your ink beforehand. You can choose your ink according to the question asked (red for

love, for example), or you can use multiple colors for the same inkromancy session to have several levels of interpretation and deepen your insights.

How the session works

Start by writing the first and last name (and date of birth if possible) of the client or person concerned on the back of the sheet. You can also write the specific question you want to have answered next to this information.

To make it easier to read later, turn the sheet over and mark it with a dot in the top left corner to determine the direction of reading when the marks are spread across your sheet. However, let intuition be your guide. Don't hesitate to turn over or rotate the drawing during your reading to better distinguish all the shapes that come to you or to study them from another angle.

You or the consultant must choose a number between the choices of 3, 7, and 13. This number will correspond to the number of drops that will be projected onto the paper. Some practitioners simply choose an odd number between 1 and 13. The choice is yours.

Focus your attention on your question and shake the ink bottle well before placing the chosen number of drops of ink on the sheet of paper using a pen or dropper. Tradition dictates that a pen should preferably be used.

Then fold your sheet of paper in four, first vertically (from top to bottom), then from right to left. Press down on the paper with your hand to spread the ink evenly, making sure that it does not soak through the paper.

Unfold your sheet of paper and interpret the results with the help of the interpretations provided on page 125.

The Ink Mirror

The Various Kinds of Mirrors in Divination

The magic of mirrors is also a vast subject, so I will try to keep it simple and restrict myself to those that involve ink. In the occult world, there are many materials that can be used as magic mirrors. The most common are silver mirrors, crystal balls, water, black obsidian mirrors, or other black witch mirrors. It can also be clear water on a dark surface, such as in a cast iron cauldron. Today, we have all kinds of mirrors, many of them often simply covered with black paint. However, their effectiveness is debatable when you consider that the traditional material used to make the background of a black magic mirror is Norwegian tar, a black, aromatic residue obtained after distilling turpentine, sometimes called pine tar. Finally, there are the mirrors on which I plan to dwell a little, those made of ink and magic.

The method of divination using ink belongs to catoptromancy.* But as we will see with the method that follows a little further on, we are close to the procedure of hydromancy, which consists of observing the behavior of "objects" thrown into water (in this case, drops of ink). The method of divination using ink and water that I propose is called ink scrying, but it is not the only method that exists. Ink can be used as a mirror in many ways. For example, you can use the palm of your hand, on which you apply a mixture of soot and oil to obtain an ink mirror. Or you can pour ink into the palm of the consultant's hand during

*Divination using mirrors.

the divination session. In Nordic and Scandinavian practices, the preferred methods involve water. Some beliefs recommend using clear water to make predictions and see into the future, and black water to connect and talk to spirits, ancestors, and the deceased.

This latter is a mixture of water and magic ink. The amount to be mixed may vary depending on whether you want a simple prediction or an answer to a question about the future, but a few drops of ink should be enough, as having a large quantity of clear water makes it easier to interpret the patterns that appear. This is the method I suggest here, as I consider it the simplest way to begin mirror divination. However, it is possible to add more black ink to the water to make it darker, or even make it completely black, giving you an entirely black mirror.

It is important to point out, and even stress, that black water is not only used for divination. It is used as an ally in rituals of banishment, protection, purification, or counter-spells, as we have seen previously. It is also used in certain funeral rites and celebrations of ancestors. Black water, like magic ink (without water), can in some cases be used to block a mirror (usually silver) and act as a barrier to a portal that you want to keep closed. In each case, the magic ink will be carefully created and ritualized. Witches and wizards will add little secrets, precious ingredients, or powerful intentions—nothing is left to chance in the creation of fluidic capacitors and magical allies.

Before discussing the divination method that uses the ink mirror in detail, I would like to outline a few principles that I apply before each divination session with ink and water, as they will also be useful in other magical or divinatory practices. The element of water, as in the rituals described above, acts as an energy portal to other planes, particularly the astral plane. I always imagine that my body acts as an anchor in matter, but that part of my consciousness and spirit is preparing to travel.

What helps me personally:

- I try to only practice divination or magic when I am in a stable emotional and mental state. If necessary, I don't hesitate to get myself "in the right frame of mind" using meditation, time to myself, breathing exercises, a walk in nature, or other grounding techniques. This helps facilitate access to an altered state of consciousness and ensure the effectiveness of the session.
- I always allow myself a few seconds of silence, breathing evenly to center myself before beginning the session.
- If it is relevant to your beliefs, you may seek the support, protection, and blessing of your guides, angels, deities, or the energies that accompany you. This is by no means an obligation, and it depends, of course, on what you are undertaking.
- Whenever possible, I try to create a mystical atmosphere around me that will be conducive to divination, for example by using natural incense, mist, candles, and so forth.
- Whether I am sitting or standing, I always make sure that my legs are uncrossed and my feet are flat on the floor to ground myself and allow energy to flow freely through my body.

- I talk to myself in my mind. Before I begin, I say phrases such as, "You are grounded in the here and now, thanks to your body. Your body will bring you back to the material world but let your mind drift away now on the course of time and travel into the astral plane. Observe, feel, and come back. Everything is clear, tell me what you see."

Materials for Divination with Ink and Water

- Black ink or ink of the color of your choice. Commercially available India ink will do, but I encourage you to use your own personalized ink or to ritualize your ink beforehand. You can choose the color based on the question asked (red for love, for example), or you can use multiple colors for the same session to get several levels of meaning and deepen your interpretations.
- A hollow, transparent container, preferably white or clear, so you can better see the shapes the ink makes and get clearer visions. This can be a deep plate (at least 1 or 2 cm deep) or a salad bowl (which is deeper), but bear in mind that depending on the depth and size of the surface, you will be working in two dimensions (with the plate) or three dimensions (with a deeper surface). For this divination practice, as for certain rituals, it is also possible to use a silver surface such as a traditional mirror.
- Tap water, spring water, or moon water, depending on your needs, possibilities, or beliefs. You can adjust as necessary.

- A feather or dropper on or in which to place your drops of ink.
- A candle in a color appropriate to the context: purple for divination, white or black for protection, red if the session is dedicated to love, and so on. You can coat it with magical oil and carve a symbol related to your intentions or your request.
- If you wish, you can ritualize your divination session by, for example, opening your session with a formula and working within a magic circle (the latter allowing you to channel, direct, and strengthen energies, while ensuring effective protection).

Divination Method

1. Light the candle.
2. Fill your container with water. Wait for the water to settle so that you can better observe the movements of the ink.
3. Shake the ink bottle well before use.
4. Place a single drop of ink in the center of your container. If you have your own preferred number of drops, I have found that a single drop is often enough to form large spots and clear shapes, while several drops quickly darken the water and leave little room for the fluid movement that ink spots form. In any case, you can interpret the first drop and then add one or two more (even different colors) to refine your interpretation.

5. Unlike paper, water is mobile. While on paper you will interpret fixed stains, with water you will interpret moving shapes, like a film. It is a scene that will unfold before your eyes.

Animals, faces, symbols, or letters are only some of the wide variety of shapes that can appear. Trust your intuition. Ink, especially in water, evolves and will often show you several things. Regardless of the method used, let the keywords come to mind. If the interpretation does not come instinctively, write down the keywords that came to you when you saw the shapes appear on a piece of paper at the end of the session. You can return to their interpretation and symbolism later.

In addition to the "visions" that will form with a depth effect, you will probably see a thin film forming on the surface of the water at the end of the session when the ink has stopped moving. You can take this into account in your interpretation, seeing it as a metaphor for the "movie screen" you have just been watching.

Coding System

When I first started working with the divinatory arts, I was looking for ways to dispel my doubts about the relevance of my interpretations, to trust my intuition completely, and to back up my interpretations. In cartomancy, there are several reading grids that provide a framework for interpretation. But this is not the case for divination methods using ink. This is the reason why I am sharing with you the "coding system" that I developed. It helped me a lot when I was just starting out. It helped me see things more clearly, but you are not obliged to use it in your practice. It is really entirely up to you whether you consider using it or not.

Imagine your medium (bowl, plate, paper) as a dial that you can divide into four equal parts. The center is the reference point. The upper half represents developments, changes, and results. The lower half represents blockages, fears, personal things, and aspects that are hidden. The right half represents the future, and the left half represents the past. The first right quarter is the "positive" future or what will be auspicious; the second right quarter is the "negative" future. The first left quarter represents the useful, positive past that can help, that has been favorable. The second left quarter is the negative past, revealing the difficulties of the past, the obstacles, the things we need to free ourselves from.

While the ink is moving about your dial surface, take into consideration the direction in which the shape is developing. As a general rule, all movement is important in magical acts.

The clockwise direction is used in witchcraft to open and attract. In divination, it can be interpreted as what comes to us, what we attract, or what is likely to happen.

The counterclockwise direction is a movement used in witchcraft to close, repel, or ward off. In divination, it can be interpreted, for example, as what is moving away from us, what we are repelling, or what we are in the process of losing.

Interpretations

Here are several interpretations of images that often emerge in divinatory practices using ink. Based on certain shapes, symbols, images, drawings, animals, and so on that you will see appearing before your eyes during your workings, you will be able to deduce the answer to the questions that have been passed on or perceive the messages that have been transmitted. Consider the shape and condition of the pictures that appear with the ink. They can give you clues about positive and favorable or negative and unfavorable trends in the message and let you home in on the meaning of the interpretation. For example, a well-drawn heart will not be interpreted in the same way as a heart that appears broken or torn. The shape or design may also seem incomplete but still evoke something for you. For example, if you see an animal appear, but not its entire body. Or if you only see half of a shape or face. You can take this into account in your interpretation. Half a face, for example, may indicate that part of the personality is not showing or that there is a hidden side. A sketch of an animal portrait may convey the animal's message or wisdom. But seeing its entire body or observing a movement may give you additional information. We will look at some examples a little later.

When you observe the marks made by your ink let the keywords that describe them come to mind instinctively. Where one person sees a cross, others will see wings or a butterfly. It is precisely these differences that will make each divination session unique. Let your intuition guide you and allow spontaneity to take over.

Classic Shapes

A face, a human appearance: observe its position and how it is moving to guide your interpretation of it. If there are several silhouettes, see if they are turning toward each other or if, on the contrary, they seem to be moving away from each other. Observe their attitude and their distribution on the paper. Is it a friendly face? Sad? A skull?

A tree: strength, anchoring, roots, ancestors, protection, things that are solid.

A tower: confusion, pride, difficulties, things being scattered, danger, unpleasant surprises, bad omens.

An umbrella: warning, caution, taking a step back, mistrust, things on the outside from which protection is required.

Rings (two separate ones): union, marriage, closeness.

An anchor: escape, departure, travel, the sea, a sign of attachment or detachment (depending on whether it is right side up or upside down).

A tooth: health, abuse, fears.

An egg: fertility, fruitfulness, birth, plans for the future.

A heart: the emotional realm, love, relationships.

A flower: blossoming, spring, talents, harmony, fertility, new beginnings (projects, ideas, wishes).

A feather: anything related to writing, messages, receiving news, transmission, means of communication, learning, exchanges.

Roots: the past, ancestors, karma, things that need to be revisited.

An arrow: going into action, the direction to follow, aiming higher, having expectations, stepping out of your comfort zone, being combative.

The crescent moon: mysteries, what is hidden, secrets, the feminine side of things, gentleness, the magic of the night, the world of dreams, mysticism.

The sun: luck, power, health, abundance, prosperity, protection.

A star: protection, success, "lucky star," rebirth, hope, blessing, truth, the right path to follow, the presence and protection of a deceased loved one, your angels, or guides close to you.

A hat: what we decide to wear, the decisions to be made, the protections to be put in place. The wrongs we do to others or that are done to us.

Scales: balance, harmony, fairness.

A beard: masculinity, virility, courage, wisdom.

Flames: passion, things beyond your control, things with destructive potential, home, family.

A mouth: encounters, things that are said, love, slander.

A wheel: luck, new cycles, things that are in motion, moving forward, things that change.

A cross: blockages, things that are at a standstill, going in the wrong direction, obstacles, prevention, jealousy.

A triangle/pyramid: protection, observation, attention, elevation.

A circle: the cycle, the absence of a beginning and an end, spinning around in circles, repetition. If, on the contrary, it looks like a sphere or a dot, the absence of angles or empty space can provide an affirmative answer.

A square: limits, foundations, constructions.

A knife or other sharp object: betrayal, dispute, separation, bad omen.

An hourglass: time, slowing down, taking time into consideration.

A ladder: moving forward slowly but surely, steps taken, success or failure, material and/or spiritual elevation.

An eye: protection, observation, the evil eye, jealousy.

Wings: growth, taking flight, leaping into the unknown, succeeding on one's own, blessing, angels, support.

A claw: primal instincts, self-defense, beastliness.

A hand: support, the future, protection against the evil eye.

Bones: death, the dead, health, poor conditions, obstacles, lack.

Animal Shapes

A butterfly: transformation, metamorphosis, independence, fulfillment, instability, ephemeral things.

A bird: news, means of communication and exchange, outside help, allies, events that run their own course.

A spider: fate, what depends on us, what we weave, withdrawal, introspection.

A snake: sexual energy, vital energy, what lies ahead, passion, fears, dangers, poison, vices, things that are brewing and cannot be seen.

A fish: emotions, abundance, the rough-and-tumble side of life.

A beetle: fertility, protection, power, happiness, the animal that guides the dead.

A rabbit: abundance, quickness, fruitfulness, spring.

A dog: faithfulness, loyalty, companionship, emotional support.

A cat: independence, vitality, autonomy, protection.

A horse: movement, freedom, purity.

A deer: protection, strength, confidence, sacred masculinity.

A wolf: loyalty, endurance, freedom.

An elephant: wisdom, knowledge, making good choices.

A giraffe: seeing the big picture, temperance, observation.

A tortoise: longevity, ancestors, discernment.

A bat: the night world, the path of initiation, the intermediary between the worlds.

An octopus: adaptability, the ability to become one with your environment, the strength of mental and physical flexibility.

Creatures

Mermaid: seduction, desires, fine words, deception, sensuality.

Phoenix: rebirth, transformation, overcoming trials, coming back stronger.

Ghosts: things that are invisible, the presence of a deceased person at your side, the feeling of being transparent, impotency, entities, being haunted by certain thoughts.

Fairy: daydreaming, imagination, creativity, connection to nature.

Goblin or Leprechaun: connection to the earth, luck, home, family.

Golem: or troll or any other kind of scary giant. Indicates taking control of things, the battle to be waged, the demons to be faced.

Symbols

In inkromancy in particular, symbols sometimes form with ink stains. It would be impossible for me to list them all, as there are so many. Here are some examples of those that have already appeared during my divination sessions.

The ankh cross: symbol of connection to the source of eternal life, truth, spiritual wisdom, divine protection, immortality, and union of the sacred feminine and the sacred masculine. It is associated with fertility, love, the divine, and humans who perform the miracle of creating life. It also refers to the key to understanding, knowledge, the key to wisdom and power, the key to solving the mysteries of life and death.

A triskelion: symbol of movement, peace, and harmony, protec tion, and good luck.

The Triple Moon: a symbol of magic, it embodies the feminine through the faces of the triple goddess. Represented by the young woman or the virgin, the mother or the adult, the elder or the oldest.

The infinity symbol: this is a symbol of balance, harmony, movement, eternity, universal knowledge, and cycles. It also represents spirituality, wisdom, creativity, expansion, and the universe. It is the image of the union between the physical and the spiritual. It is also linked to time.

Yin and yang: symbol of interdependence, balance, intuition, creativity, interconnection, or as a representation of the male-female couple.

Runes

Runes are graphic symbols that can be easily incorporated into divination practices with ink. Here is a very brief interpretation of each rune in divination.

Fehu: beginning, movement, impulse, wealth, abundance, fertility, money. It is often linked to work, to physical or material prosperity, instinct, the struggle for something, romantic conquest, or the spirit of conquest.

Uruz: wisdom, reflection, time for integration, inspiration, meditation, seeking help, gestation, birth, and the maternal aspect. Things we ruminate on, withdrawal into oneself.

Thurisaz: strength and violence, what hurts, something that stings and causes pain like a thorn. Also connected with shock, confrontation, hostility, moral or physical brutality, primal forces, combat, and thorny problems.

Ansuz: speech, the mouth, breath, thought, learning, mental abilities, intelligence, knowledge, consciousness, education, or anything related to childhood and maturity. Listening or not listening.

Raidho: symbol of progress. The journey, order, the trip, the cycle, the path, the process, transport, moving from one point to another. But also transformation, both of the individual and of all forms of energy.

Kenaz: light in darkness, transmutation, understanding, compassion, energetic stability, mastery, and controllable fire. Learning, knowledge, and the development of our abilities.

Gebo: rune of the gift, of the present, the link rune that symbolizes union, connections, but also hospitality, generosity, luck, exchange, sharing, harmony, cooperation, associations, and love.

Wunjo: friendship, camaraderie, clan, family, our identity, shared things, well-being, and victory. Our ability to integrate, to find our place or not. It is a rune of stability.

Hagalaz: associated with the link between human consciousness and other planes, but also with bad weather (both literal and figurative), rupture, confusion, and restructuring. It can sometimes indicate a delay in events.

Nauthiz: the duty to free oneself from a constraint, to overcome something that seemed to be a need, often created by an absence or a fear. The rune of challenge.

Isa: the static force that, once in motion, proves to be very powerful. Symbolizes observation, rupture, study of our inner self, or refocusing on oneself.

Jera: positive completion, happiness, generosity, the benefits reaped after effort, hard work, or sacrifice. It is a rune that refers to the cycles of the seasons, natural balance, and the mystical link between heaven and earth.

Eihwaz: a passage, a path of evolution, transformation, and liberation that sometimes involves a form of initiatory death. It therefore evokes the upheavals, turmoil, and questioning that can result from this.

Perthro: the uncertainties of fate, which should not be seen as inevitable but rather as an active force. It symbolizes pleasure, providence, intuition, and surprises (both good and bad).

Elhaz/Algiz: defense, refuge, blessing, support, love, strong emotional ties, trust, help, vulnerability, and protection.

Sowilo: success, achievement, triumph, self-confidence, strength, luck, and positive and fruitful relationships. It indicates external support that promotes the achievement of our goals.

Tiwaz: activity, triumph, courage, the notion of sacrifice, a form of constructive regulation, but also positive forces in action. Success in projects undertaken, attraction, active sexuality, or a beneficial encounter or experience.

Berkano: rune of mystery and enigma, feminine principles and life, fertility, beginning, growth in the broadest sense, but also birth or a period conducive to procreation. It indicates that the ground is fertile for any form of project.

Ehwaz: movement, positive change, professional development, moving house, renewal, new beginnings or a new form of adventure. It also represents fidelity and loyalty. It may indicate a choice to be made, a decision to be taken or a change in your life.

Mannaz: this rune refers to man and humanity. It represents our loved ones, society, unity, the quest for harmony and balance, brotherhood, solidarity, and hope.

Laguz: emotions, the unconscious, intuition, and our feelings in general. As it symbolizes the vital force, it can indicate love at first sight, a sudden infatuation, or passionate love, potential instability, or emotional effervescence.

Ingwaz: fertility, expansion, explosive energy, sacred fire, the transition from gestation to birth, and the ability to achieve.

Othila: home, family, bonds within a family or group of friends, messages from ancestors, legacies, roots, or the past.

Dagaz: things will happen naturally. This rune will always bring light and positivity, such as good health or improved health, abundance and prosperity, optimism, joy, and the achievement of goals.

Numbers

Here is a brief summary of the symbolism of numbers.

1: unity, the father, masculine energy, man, spouse, the beginning, a new start, initiative, the direction to follow, leadership, kindness, or creative energy.

2: mother, feminine energy, spouse, kindness, reconciliation, ability to unite, duality, or confrontation.

3: child, creation, creativity, balance, expression, free-thinking spirit, contact, protection, trinity, or the cycle of life and nature.

4: achievement, foundations, grounding, perseverance, order, discipline, rigor, organization, maturity, boundaries, or balance.

5: discovery, freedom, independence, the breath of life, mobility, or adventure.

6: balance, sensitivity, forgiveness, acceptance, creation, fertility, family, perfection, or multiple potentials.

7: the sacred number, wisdom, personal life, interiority, spirituality, analytical ability, understanding, reflection, knowledge, faith, understanding of the world, or luck.

8: symbol of infinity, power, justice, expansion, strength of accomplishment, power, or karma.

9: elevation, fulfillment, blossoming, universal love, wisdom, integrity, transmission, clairvoyance, truth, teaching, gestation, or happiness.

Master Numbers

11: inner strength, spiritual power, intuition, the extraordinary, clairvoyance, inspiration, revelation, messages, mediumship, or magnetism.

22: Building, determination, balance, fulfillment, or ambition.

33: Strong potential, being accompanied, kindness, generosity, or help.

Several Symbols

Bind rune symbol of banishment (Raidho and Nauthiz)

Bind rune for luck

Bind rune for love

Symbol of love: Mars and Venus

Runic Seal

The Pentacle of Earth

Practical Case Examples

There is nothing better than examples to help and guide you in your first interpretations. It is through practice that we can develop ease and intuitive reflexes of expression. It is important to realize that each interpretation will be unique to the practitioner performing it. Through my perspective, we will analyze and study the interpretations of the two types of divination methods described earlier. The context and question will be the same for both sessions. These interpretations are brief examples to show you how to proceed. I will only detail what comes to mind first to give you a starting point for interpretation. But I encourage you to try for yourself with the aids mentioned above and your own intuition.

The Context and the Question Asked by the Client:

The client would like to know whether his creative and artistic professional projects will bear fruit. He wants to know whether they are worth devoting more time and personal investment to, and whether the risks involved in pursuing them will ultimately pay off.

Applied Inkromancy

For the sake of practice, take some time to look at the photos on the following pages before reading my comments. Try to let your intuition and feelings guide you before reading mine, so that you are not influenced by my personal perceptions.

Overall, I see very distinct patterns. The first thing that strikes me are the "panda eyes" at the top, a bat in the center

(which could also be the panda's nose). And finally, there are some small spots that at first glance made me think of footprints or paw prints leading outward. However, these marks could also be the panda's mouth or whiskers.

If I were to break it down, I would start with the gaze (of the panda). For me, the symbolism of the gaze is linked to observation, the things we fix our eyes on and that hold our attention, the goal we never lose sight of, the mirror of the soul.

The bat is an animal that carries wisdom and represents the night world, the occult, the path of initiation, moving forward blindly but quickly and with exceptional personal resources. The spot in the middle caught my attention because when I looked closely, I saw a deer's head appear. Deer symbolize protection, strength, and confidence, among other things.

The footprints or paw prints leading outward suggest to me the idea of starting off, of movement. They are leaving the middle to head outward, to spring into action.

The message seems quite clear: Things are happening, and the person who came to me will make even more progress if he remains focused on his goals and invests the energy required to achieve them. The confidence and protection that deer embody can confirm that he is on the right track. The bat touches on other aspects of life besides work. He is on his initiatory path, and he will also evolve on a personal level through his projects and the new professional experiences he wishes to develop. By using the second method we can confirm if this divination session is accurate or inaccurate.

Divination by Ink and Water

Using the same question, we are going to do the first session with purple ink and the second with black ink. We will have to be satisfied here using a photo and therefore an interpretation on one specific moment in time. But keep in mind that this is like a small scene unfolding on stage, that it is in movement and thus the pictures that form continue to evolve.

The first obvious elements I see are a rather frail human form with a clearly visible face. I can also see what look like small wings taking shape in the background. They seem to rise above something while looking down at the ground. This inspires a mental image of the illustrations by the famous Nicoletta Ceccoli, who often depicts fantasy creatures with female faces, some of which are winged like fairies. The word *muse* pops into my mind, which helps to convey the creative and artistic nature of the message. Muses indicate inspiration and creativity in all things related to the arts and talents. They bring support and good energy. Fairies have a similar interpretation, as they are linked to dreams, imagination, and creativity, as well as a connection with nature and the elements. We can infer from this that the consultant has a good support network, that their muse is present at their side, and that, as a result, they will not lack for ideas, creativity, or imagination. These interpretations suggest that there is positive encouragement pushing the consultant toward this path that they have hesitations about taking.

Interpretation with purple ink.

Interpretation with black ink.

A large stain stands out and catches my attention. From a distance, I can make out what looks like a horse in profile with a curved neck. Be aware that the images, perceptions, sensations, and words that come to you are the way your intuition communicates with you. Your intuition uses memories, information, or personal experiences to convey messages to you more easily. It uses things that are part of your individual personality, your passions, your tastes, your memories, your experiences, and so forth. Speaking personally, I have a special relationship with horses, which are a passion of mine and bring back my childhood dreams. It is an animal that I admire and feel very close to. The horse is a symbol of movement, fluidity, purity, freedom, renewal, and speed. In my view, this apparition conveys these messages to the client. My personal intuition tells me that beyond the professional and artistic realm, the client will also experience spiritual as well as material growth by following this calling. Furthermore, the presence of the horse may indicate that things could move much faster for the client than he currently thinks.

My feelings and interpretations determine what I chose to emphasize in these three inkromancy divination essays. Of course, the interpretations could be explored further and the observations made more detailed in order to gain even greater insight. But this gives you some concrete examples based on a practical case study.

Appendix on Magical Rituals

Even though not all rituals are identical, there is a certain common "methodology" in high magic, as well as in most ceremonial magic and witchcraft practices.

If you cannot find a ritual that suits you, you can create your own, on condition that you feel comfortable with your practice. As a general rule, repetition and practice contribute to their effectiveness.

On the next page you will find an outline that will give you an overview of how a magical ceremony unfolds. This framework will be a useful guide, especially if you are a beginner.

General Outline to Serve as an Example

1. Start by preparing your altar and collecting your tools.
2. Next purify your sacred space (smudging the space or using incense, for example). Be in a stable emotional state to perform your magic; relax if necessary and cleanse yourself energetically. Most often, witches and wizards take a ritual bath beforehand to do this.
3. Begin by opening the magic circle (which is the gateway between this world and the higher worlds).
4. Invoke the elements and/or energies, the deities.
5. Perform the ritual act, during which you condense, channel, and transform energies (using mantras, magic phrases, your magical creations, and so on).
6. Project these energies (this is called "casting the spell").
7. Thank the elements, angels, or deities you have called upon, then close the circle.

Additional Tips

- Choose the right moment to perform a magical act (days, astrological influences, moon phases, etc.). This is important for many rituals. The prosperity ritual, for example, is best performed on Thursday, the day of Jupiter.
- Hold tight to your precious critical faculties. Even if no one can tell you what you should do or how to do it, remind

yourself that all magic first passes through your mind and your consciousness, and that it is your intention that will guide your will. Don't hesitate to question your motivations for performing a magical act. All esoteric practices must be performed with awareness. All magical currents work in accordance with the laws of the universe and do not violate them. Practice in harmony with yourself, be conscious of your will, probe the reasons for your desire, know where your motivation comes from, and analyze your emotional state. It is very important to be aware of the real reasons that prompt us to cast a spell or perform a magical act.

- Choose your materials, ingredients (herbs, incense, candles, etc.), magic phrases, and energies with which to work carefully. All of this will determine the effectiveness of your spells.
- At the end of your magical ceremony, don't hesitate to perform another energy cleansing to remove any residual energies without waiting for your next ritual.

Acknowledgments

To my family and friends for their support and encouragement, which keep me going.

To my editor and the entire team at Éditions Bussière, I am so delighted to be working with you.

To the magic of ink, so powerful! It encouraged me to share this book with you. It reminded me that ink allows words to be passed on and made immortal.

To the magicians, witches, and practitioners of esotericism who came before us. They knew how to preserve occult knowledge and magical practices through the ages.

To you who have read these lines. You who will pass them on in turn.

Thank you from the bottom of my heart.

Find Noémie Myara
On Instagram: **@myeimeon**
In her shop: **https://www.etsy.com/fr/shop/MyEimeon**

Bibliography

Bardon, Franz. *Initiation into Hermetics: The Path of the True Adept.* Merkur Pub Co, 2011.

Chanceland. *La magie des huiles et des encens.* Ed. Bussière, 2015.

Lauvergne, Vincent. *Traité des encens.* Trajectoire, 2018.

Lecouteux, Claude. *Le livre des talismans et des amulettes.* Imago, 2005.

———. *The High Magic of Talismans and Amulets.* Inner Traditions, 2014.

Manassé, Benjamin. *Rituel de magie blanche.* Ed. Bussière 1998.

Mordock, Zoran. *Le livre des talismans et l'art de la nigromancie.* N.p., n.d.

Myara, Noémie. *Autels et pentacles de sorcières.* Secret Etoiles, 2021.

———. *Le guide des symboles magiques.* Secret D'étoiles, 2024.

———. *Le guide des runes.* Secret D'étoiles, 2022.

Soror DS et Spartakus Freeman. *Sceaux et talismansles—les sigil.* Ed. Bussière 2014.

Vici, Luce. *Les taches d'encre. Symbolisme et interpretation.* Éditions Niclaus, 1936.

Index